ISSUE 2

Published by 404 INK

404INK.COM   HELLO@404INK.COM
FACEBOOK: /404INK **TWITTER:** @404INK
SUBSCRIBE: PATREON.COM/404INK

ISBN: 978-0-9956238-4-2
Ebook: 978-0-9956238-5-9
ISSN: 2399-1577

Managing editors: Heather McDaid & Laura Jones
Cover design: Michaela @ SOB Design

Printed by Bell & Bain

CONTENTS

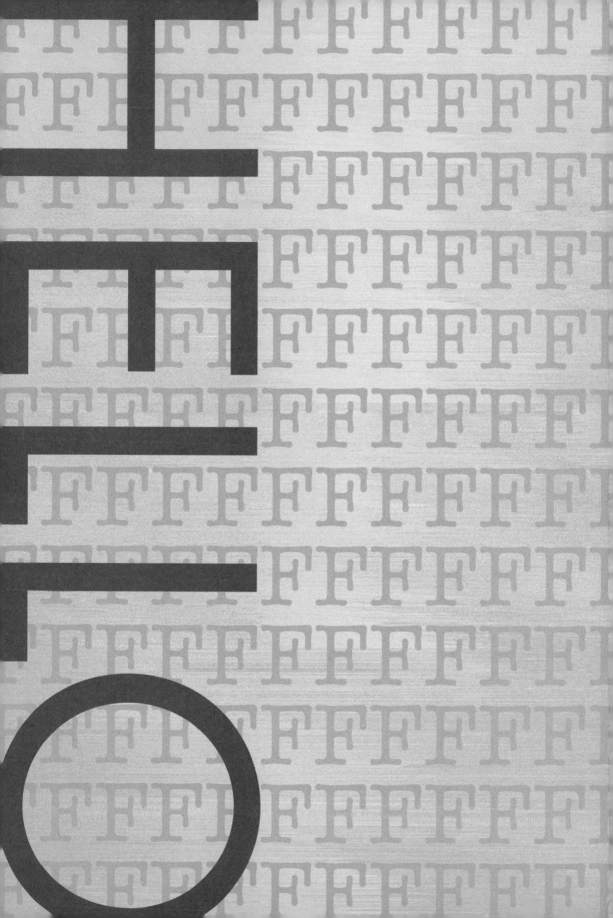

HELLO.
AGAIN.
WE'RE BACK.
DID YOU MISS US?

A lot has happened since Issue 1 of 404 Ink's very first literary magazine. It went to print a week before the American Presidential election in November 2016 and we thought, 'You know what would be a good idea? Let's put a flowchart about the outcome of the election'. The upside is that the flowchart still works well as it ages. The downside is the reminder that our 'buy books to build a book fort for your safety' answer just makes you feel a little sad when you realise what actually happened and who, at the moment of this magazine going to print in May 2017, is currently sitting in the White House (or his own very gold-plated house, who knows?)

It's fair to say the new US President has inspired a lot of F-word laced discussions and this second issue of 404 Ink is little different. While difficult to ignore, it's not all about the Presidency. We wanted this issue to explore very relevant elements of confrontation but we also want to create a little refuge from current affairs, and we've got quite a range to take temporary shelter in.

You can't move for the F-words. Some rude, some brimming with fight, some a little more subtle.

Fatigue.

Flesh.

'Facts'.

Fear.

Feces...

Farewells.

You might have to really look for the F-word in some of the following pieces but believe us, they're there. Happy f*%king hunting.

– Heather & Laura
Directors of 404 Ink

SOUNDING OFF

SOUNDING OFF
꽃 이야기

JEN BURROWS

I'm learning a language
without any f-words.
There's no acoustic for it:
no sound that asks you
to take your bottom lip
in your teeth and bite down.
If I told you I feel the same
in a borrowed tongue,
would it sound strange?
All my old fears
and well-worn fantasies
are falling out of form
　　　－ shifting and stretching out,
screwing up and sounding off －
　　　flexing and flickering and flooding in
until my own words lose meaning
and there's only the feelings
turning tangible on my new tongue －
kissing my bottom lip
and flowering out
my open mouth.

SANS

LINGUA FRANCA

SANS LINGUA FRANCA

THOMAS WELSH

Imagine being able to save the world with just a few specific words. Now imagine every man, woman, and child is unable to understand those words. Such is my plight. Such is the plight of our species.

I know not why I write this. Perhaps in hope more than expectation, I desire that someone will stumble on this final journal entry. If you are that someone then welcome to my home and it is good to know you. Congratulations – you have already stumbled on the cure. I can explain how to ensure your present state of salvation is permanent. But not quite yet. Please read to the end. All will be made clear.

Fear not, I will be brief, and the information I offer will undo the SLF bacterium's effects completely. My only wish is that I could have spoken to you in person. Alas, our enemy was canny. His first attack disabled the only weapon we could use to defeat him. Our words.

Before I divulge the information you need to evade the grasp of this insidious affliction, let me first tell you about how I found my transient salvation. Let me tell you about The Girl.

Her real name I do not know. If she possessed one, there was no way she could communicate it to me. But she was the closest thing to a success I encountered. I called her Eve.

She was huddled. Her knees were pulled up tight to her chest as if any limb extended in my direction would be in danger. Of what I wondered? Probably – most likely – she expected me to take a bite out of her. Certainly it would be her most probable fate if any other man had trapped her in a basement like this. The common courtesy of 'not eating your guests' is a dying tradition in these uncivilized times.

I had to wait. The longer she spent there – trapped but safe – the more likely she was to accept that I had no ill intentions. There was simply no other way to communicate my benign plan. A simple request – 'please take these pills' – was not so simple at all. To win her trust I'd have to allay her fears and assure her I meant no harm. But I also had to be firm.

Suffice it to say every day since the outbreak had been tremendously vexing for me. I am not unaware of the irony: a former Professor of Linguistics unable to communicate with anyone, and sharing that affliction with the rest of humanity. Still, I could not stop my mind thinking that same utterly un-useful thought over and over: *if only there was some way to talk to Eve*. Of course, that was the whole problem. For me, for her, and for every single other remaining man, woman and child grunting at each other indecipherably on this maddeningly noisy, green and blue sphere. This planet with a billion voices and no talking.

Eve shivered and cried. The most relatable actions she performed, and the only behavior of hers that I could understand. I wondered whether soon even our most primal behaviors would no longer be comprehensible to one another. The pathogen had certainly progressed since its first appearance ten years prior. At first, it had caused no more than stuttering and confusion amongst victims. Misplaced words. Rearranged grammar. It had almost been comical, the way it had twisted our speech into a child-like soup of mixed words and noises. But it progressed quickly. Within a few weeks there was not a single soul on the planet who could string together a sentence that anyone else could understand.

And worst of all I had (and have) the awful sense that every moment our shared affliction worsens. The thin threads of understanding between each of us are fraying further each day. How can we maintain basic empathy when our behaviors are utterly alien to one another? That's right, not just our words. Not just our language and writing. Any and all forms of expression which might elicit empathy or understanding are obscured. That's how insidious this accursed brain bug is.

Let me give you an example. How do you express sadness? For me, water runs from my eyes. Does this sound odd to you? For you, perhaps sadness is denoted by bent knees or a trembling lip or blinking. How do you greet a friend? At one time, I would raise an arm in the air and move it back and forth. You? Do you rotate your left foot, or twitch your nose or walk backwards in a circle? Each of us – each and every one – has had our brains rewired to make our interaction rituals different. This nasty plague has made us a planet of creatures unable to agree on any basic forms of interaction. Beyond the simplest. We all run, we all fight and we all eat. But that is all and that is not enough. When you can no longer speak to the lady in the grocery stores to buy a tin of beans, it's amazing how quickly you will consider eating her instead of the beans. Especially when the shelves are bare and there are no more beans in the entire world.

Have no doubt, my new friend, for each and every one of us the most dangerous thing we encounter in this new reality is another person.

So this girl – ah yes, Eve I am supposed to call her – was afraid. I had snatched

Eve from a distant location. I'd fortified this old townhouse and I knew the area around it well, but no one would come within half a mile of my sanctum. My pipe-rifle had seen off too many scavengers and ferals. My home truly was my castle. But it was a remote and lonely one.

I had trapped my... do I say victim? Subject? The word doesn't matter I suppose. It had been easy to catch The Girl. I had no wish to kidnap a woman, but – and I hesitate to admit this – I was glad my subject had been a skinny young girl rather than a burly, meat-starved, sharp-toothed feral male. Judge me however you see fit.

I snatched her in the night, much as a true villain might. I am old, and no doubt youth is a great asset, but in the land of the malnourished, the well-fed man is king. I was far too strong for her. Afterwards, I felt every bit the monster I must have resembled.

But I had work to do. And by 'work', I mean the long, difficult process of winning her trust. I offered her food. Good food this time. A stew made of rat's meat and carrots and onions with fresh garlic and chili. She devoured it ravenously. I gave her clothes. Warm ones: furs and woolen sweaters, scavenged from a well-to-do families abode. She was wary of them at first, but after the first cold night closed in, I found her wearing them the next morning.

I feel your frustration, dear reader. You want to know of the cure for the SLF bacterium. Trust me, I will get you there. First, let me tell you how I chanced upon it. Hold Eve in your mind, we shall return to her in a moment.

Long before I met The Girl, I explored far and wide. For many years I travelled. I found nothing that offered me hope for our future. When the time came for my pilgrimage to end I had found not a single human who could talk to me, nor I to them. I had lost hope and I was feeling rather forlorn and dejected and – I have to confess – I was thinking of doing myself in. You see, I'd witnessed a somewhat horrible act done to a baby and its mother and that was quite enough for me. Old Albert Camus had said the only serious philosophical question was whether one should commit suicide, and I had come down firmly in the affirmative.

So already committed to my fate, I resolved to indulge some of my baser desires before I left this world. I hope you won't think less of me, but I have committed to a deep truth rather than a rose-tinted version of my exploits.

I sought to escape to the shopping mall and eat candy and ice cream from the cinema concession stand, steal alcohol wherever I could find it and hopefully find some pornographic photographs in the arts section of the book store. At the end of my binge session and with all my base urges satisfied, I ended up in a pharmacy where I feasted on a myriad of drugs, popping pills at random and hoping that I'd either get some sort of high, or better yet find a painless end to a painful life.

I know not how long I was there, but at one point I wandered out into the main atrium of the mall. And then it happened. The most confusing, glorious moment of my life to date. 'Cola.' That's what the sign read. And I understood it. Cola. And there in the window I saw little tin cans filled with black, bubbly liquid. That was cola. The word and the meaning and the object all lined up in my head. And they corresponded with reality.

I'm not sure there's any way to express the feeling you get when you lose something so valuable then get it back. You feel two things mainly, one positive and one negative. On the positive, you feel the joy. It's back. My old life came back. I never thought it would.

But then there's the fear. The fear that the reprieve is temporary. That you'll lose everything all over again.

But oh the joy! I read writing on candy wrappers. The signs in the stores. The names on the old, faded movie posters. Getting my language back gave me a reason to live, but it also gave me a goal. I had to speak with another person. Tell a joke and hear someone laugh. That was my mission now. And to do that, my simple, impossible task was to make someone take the same pills I had taken.

And so we are back in that basement. Me and Eve. Three days of tempting and coaxing her to try the pills. To take one freely and of her own volition. I pleaded, I joked, I tempted, I asked politely, I asked firmly, I pointed, I nodded, I coaxed, I cried. None of it worked. Until one day, for reasons only she under-stood, as I stood there picking dirt from my nails, she crawled across the floor, looked up at me with eyes free of fear or expectation, and opened her mouth. Without hesitation and before I could process what was happening fully, I dropped a handful of pills into her mouth. She crunched and swallowed them without water, then crawled back to her corner and sat and looked at me. From that point on she no longer avoided my gaze.

That night we didn't speak, but we both felt the change. In our posture, in the way we looked at one another and in the way we… moved? Breathed? There was a… synchronization. It was as if, by slow degrees, our frequencies were being tuned to match one another. It was an oddly intimate thing.

After that night things changed between me and Eve. I made a big show of unlocking the door to the basement. I gestured at the exit to show her she could leave. She made no move to do so.

And she took more of the pills. She came to me, mouth open, ready to swallow them every four hours. After the fifth dose, she made a noise. Of course, that is not rare. We are all making noises all the time now. The remarkable thing about this noise was that it sounded like a word to me. A word I recognised. 'Hello'. Or something like it. With its utterance my equilibrium was utterly tipped – unbalanced and twisted and I was impossibly reborn. As a person. For you see, what I'd come to realise is that when we cannot communicate with other people, we cease to be *people* at all. What is a single person when there are no other people to recognize them as such? So when Eve said 'hello' I was quite literally revived. I was back from the dead, and we were the last (and first) *people* in the whole world.

Those weeks were long and easy. Her language did not come back like mine – in a flash – but rather it came in degrees. A word at a time, sometimes two words in a day. Her writing was faster than her speech. Perhaps her throat forgot how to make the sounds. But in a month, Eve could write me notes I could read, and I was able to say words she recognised. Words like 'hope' and 'friend' and even 'thank you.'

So if my mission was a success, why did I write this journal, you may ask. What is its purpose? Shouldn't Eve and I be out saving people, one at a time, re-educating the world on the simple combination of everyday medications that will cure them of the SLF bacterium?

Perhaps you have already fathomed our fate. It seems there is something special about me. My reaction to the treatment was so much greater than hers. In fact, I regained my powers of language as quickly as Eve lost hers. She gained a word or two a day for three months, but when the pendulum swung back and she started to lose them again, they departed at a much quicker rate.

I would thank you not to ask me for *details*, dear reader. The progress of her renewed illness was quick enough to be frightening, but slow enough to be agonizing. I try not to think on it. Just as I try not to think of how Eve left this world. Filled with despair, unable to deal with the pain of losing her humanity twice. Suffice it to say, I miss her dearly.

And I fear I shall join her soon. You might have guessed it, but this is more than a journal entry, but also much less. There shall be no more notes after this one. This final note. I trust you understand my meaning.

And though I am confident no one else will find this message, I am not beyond hope. Not for you anyway, dear reader. If you are fucking reading this dis nis, you truly knead to know no no more than what those ose pills are. You will laugh arf aff. The cure to your affliction iction action is as simple as bas thra s no gorya az garden gorya.

Semetridon Natama Sadaya.

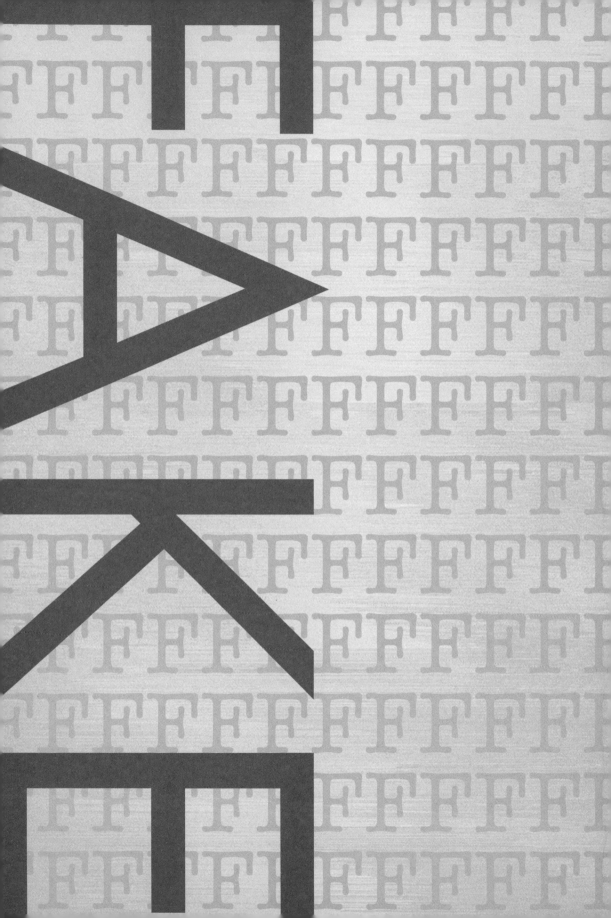

FAKE

10 VARIATIONS ON 10 WORDS

MICHAEL STEPHENSON

Fiction is the lie through which we tell the truth.
Albert Camus

Fiction is the lie through which we tell the truth.
We tell the truth though the lie which is fiction.
We tell the truth through the lie. Which is fiction?
Which fiction is the lie we tell the truth through?
Which is the truth we tell through fiction, the lie?
Through fiction, the lie, we tell which is the truth.
Lie through the fiction. We tell which is the truth.
We tell – through the lie, the fiction – the truth.
We tell the lie – the fiction – through the truth.
Truth is the fiction through which we tell the lie.

FOR BOOKS' SAKE

CHAMPIONING WRITING BY WOMEN

FOR BOOKS' SAKE
'JUST FUCKING DO IT'

Our mission is to create a community that centres, supports and champions writing by women, challenging inequality and empowering women and girls of all backgrounds to tell their stories and have their voices heard.

It's a simple concept, but a powerful one. For Books' Sake's goal to support writing by women takes many forms: podcasts, reviews, weekend reads, partnering with Write Like A Grrrl to run courses, publishing anthologies, hosting events like That's What She Said and their Grrrl Con conference, to name a handful.

So the obvious question: why focus on women and girls? 'Media audits like the VIDA Count have shown that women writers don't get the coverage they deserve in the mainstream media,' explains founder Jane Bradley. 'Major literary prizes, festivals and exam board syllabi have historically been and continue to be consistently dominated by men (and typically educated, white, hetero men at that). We wanted to address and counteract that imbalance, and provide a platform so that all these incredible women writers can connect, support and celebrate each other.

'Whether it was published women writers struggling to reach readers or emerging women writers struggling to develop their skills and experience, we wanted to support them and create opportunities for them to showcase their voices and skills. Projects like Halo, The Fem Lit Mag, Dear Damsels, Silver Press, The Chapess and Salome magazine all do an incredible job of this too – none of these were around when we started in 2010 but we're thrilled to be in such fantastic company now!'

For Books' Sake are tireless in offering opportunities – it isn't just about boosting authors that are already there, but giving women the tools to become a writer

At the That's What She Said *Nasty Women* launch, March 2017. Photo by Kyle McGurk.

themselves, regardless of their starting point. Whether they've been writing for years or just fancy trying it out, they're on hand.

'I honestly believe it can be revolutionary to get women writers together, sharing ideas, advice and resources,' she enthuses. 'It's helped my own writing progress far beyond what I would have been able to achieve in isolation, so being able to facilitate that for other women writers is a true honour. Writing can be an isolating, intimidating endeavour, especially for women who may be facing any number of barriers. Getting support and company to make that journey less lonely and more enjoyable is half the battle – and means more women progressing further, which is what we're all about.'

As a volunteer-led organisation, they've managed to become a vital resource for writers. Their online features roll on, bringing dazzling new writing to new audiences week by week, so there's no rest due any time soon. In June, they partner with Write Like A Grrrl again to run the second Grrrl Con, a three-day extravaganza of talks, workshops and performers. Then August 16th – 26th they're bringing their renowned spoken word night That's What She Said up to the Edinburgh Fringe for one hell of a party.

They rely on your support to keep going, whether that's fundraising, following them online, or just checking in to read the writing they're showcasing. While they seem to be balancing twenty million things at once, they do it with style, and it's an added bonus for them that it's so rewarding.

'Seeing women and girls develop trust and confidence in their own voices, their stories, and their writing is really exciting,' says Jane. 'It's rewarding to be able to see that development in action, and to feel like we've played a part in helping make it happen.

'I'd be remiss if I didn't mention how incredible it is to work with some of the more established women writers we've collaborated with too; Denise Mina spoke at last year's Grrrl Con, all about punk, and privilege, and how you have to 'just fucking do it.' It might have been the fact I'd been awake since 4am but listening to that moved me to tears, and it was just so special to be with my Grrrl Con co-organisers Kerry Ryan and Claire Askew and a hundred other women writers, getting that encouragement and validation from such an iconic author.'

So, in the spirit of Denise Mina's talk from last year: thinking of writing? Just fucking do it. If you're looking for where to start, we know the perfect place.

FBS' TOP RECENT BOOKS BY WOMEN

A Beginner's Guide to Losing Your Mind by Emily Reynolds; an incredibly brave, bold, frank and funny personal account of being diagnosed with bipolar, with practical advice for young people struggling with their mental health, as well as those around them.

The Girls by Emma Cline; bittersweet and beautiful, this is an absolutely entrancing debut novel, and an ideal summer read.

We Go Around in the Night and Are Consumed by the Fire by Jules Grant; a heart-breaking debut novel by a former barrister about a lesbian biker gang in Manchester.

As In Judy by Rosie Garland; gorgeous poetry by the gothic grande dame. Rosie is a literary legend and her latest collection is every bit as queer, political and powerful as you'd expect. Rich, evocative, immersive and intoxicating.

At the That's What She Said *Nasty Women* launch, March 2017. Photo by Kyle McGurk.

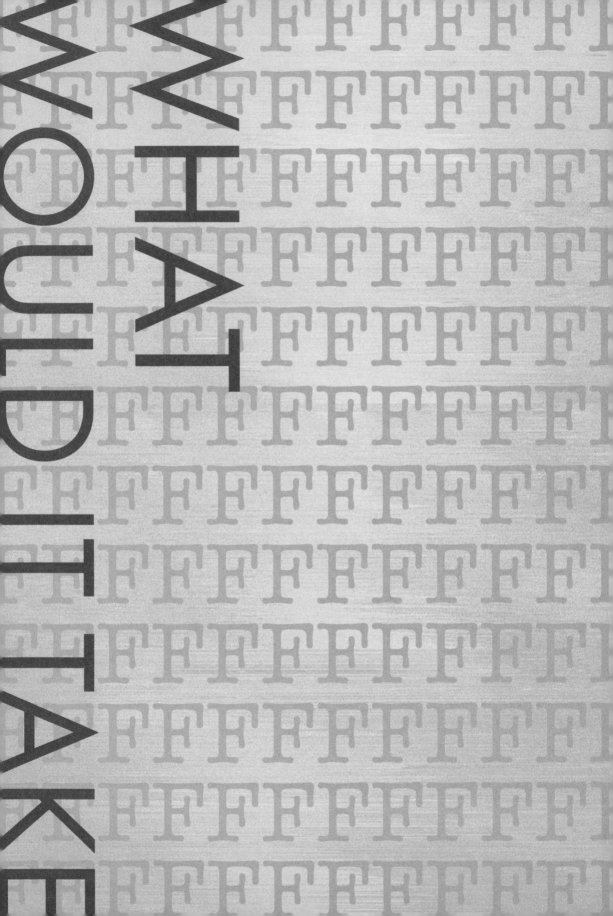

WHAT WOULD IT TAKE

ALAN FIELDEN

1. His eyes fall out and he keeps talking.

2. Brains seen in bathtubs, legs jutting from kitchen bins, lamp shades of human skin.

3. At the press conference with Xi Jinping, looking into the camera. Starts masturbating in Xi's direction. Does that shoulder shrug thing.

4. He holds up his hands at the rally;
'I have a gun. It's a tremendous gun. This is an American gun—'
The gun goes off, a baby held aloft loses half its face.

5. WikiLeaks, The Guardian, CNN, Fox News et al. run images of his reptilian feet.

6. His wife accuses him of sexual abuse. He denies the charges, calls her a 'nasty, European gold digger'. She releases a video of him threatening her with a broken bottle.

7. He is photographed in his garden without his weird hair. His scalp is a swarming mass of red ants. They co-ordinate themselves to spell out the words that pass through his mind. The word *tremendous* spelled out in red ants. The word *pussy* spelled out in red ants. The words *failure, fuck-up,* and *Father*.

8. A bullet punctures his right lung. Hospital staff gather round the bed in silence. The nurse wipes the sweat from the Head Physician's forehead. The Head Physician pulls the plug. They all nod once.

9. A letter is found, written by him as a teenager to the then object of his affections,

Sweetheart,

I think there are benefits to a capitalist system in terms of competition driving innovation, variety leading to choice, and all the individual freedoms that attend a consumer democracy.

But it seems, to me, indisputable that unregulated capitalism inevitably becomes a race amongst those who control the means of production to find any way to abuse, manipulate and exploit both their workers and their consumers. With regulation capitalism is tolerable.

That is the realist in me speaking.

The idealist says living in a capitalist society has tremendous affects on its citizens. We fetishize money and wealth beyond any intrinsic value they may possess. We learn the price of things but lose track of their worth. We are dehumanised; human interaction becomes transactional. We treat each other as services.

It's my hope that we move toward abundance rather than scarcity. Because it's resource scarcity—and I'm talking as much about food as a resource here as I am about love and generosity as resources—it's resource scarcity that begets most human evils.

Speaking of love, will you meet me beneath the peach trees on Wednesday?

x

10. Everyone — one night — disappears.

11. An audio tape emerges, '…The American people? I love the American people. The people at my rallies, I love them. They're my best friends. All of them. And—I like to think of myself as a shepherd, you know, and they're my cattle. The best cattle. And I'm going to milk them gently with my hands. One at a time, right into the bucket. Every tremendous drop. I'm going to milk them so dry, whilst they're sleeping…'

12. He is revealed to be a fictional character that has manifest itself into our world through sheer will.

13. No one can find the President for three days. He is in a West Virginian diner toilet cubicle wrapped in a shit smeared American flag. He releases a public announcement that he is 'unwell'. Due to his rapidly declining mental health his assets are divided between his family — he leaves everything to Goneril and Regan. At mandatory ('means you have to do it') breakfast workout a twinge in

the back of his head threatens to pierce his fogged psyche emerging as a full-throated scream, *I am the President of the United States of America*. He sees the look in the nurse's eyes and stops himself because he knows too well the needles and sparks.

14. He wakes up one morning inside the body of Tom Hanks like in the 1988 film *Big*. Presumably Tom Hanks has swapped bodies with his and done the decent thing.

15. He wakes up one morning inside the body of Lindsay Lohan like in the 2003 film *Freaky Friday*. Presumably Lindsay Lohan has swapped bodies with his and done the decent thing.

16. He wakes up one morning inside the body of Jennifer Garner like in the 2004 film *Going On 30*. Presumably Jennifer Garner has swapped bodies with his and done the decent thing.

17. He wakes up one morning inside the body of Hillary Clinton. He looks in the mirror and begins to laugh. He stares at himself. Strangers speak to him in a way that confuses him. One day he cries having read a hand-written letter from a twelve year old girl called Emily; the letter is supportive, it is loving, it is sincere, it is heart-breaking. He cries and the tears roll from Hilary's eyes, down Hilary's cheeks, blotting the paper. Waking from this dream disconcerted he nukes Iran.

18. He has a crisis of conscience. He buries it. He trips over a cat and cracks his skull.

FESSIONS

FISSION

HEATHER PARRY

God, you're a real piece of shit, she thinks, though she smiles, and lifts the glass of acrid wine to her mouth, and nods all the more while he bloviates about equity or partners or the rest of those business words that make her want to bite through the glass between her lips. The only thing she cares to ascertain is that some people are in vague trouble and he's fucking them over, as ever, as he always does, and that's how he can afford to buy Barolo by the bottle no matter where they're eating. She hates the stuff, it gives her acid reflux and a headache, but she likes to watch him show off as he orders, likes to watch the numbers on the bill grow bigger, knowing that it will all come up later and end its days in the bottom of her cheap, semi-unflushable toilet. Turned to excrement, mixed with the blood from her serrated throat. Of course, that's not really why she's there. How petty, how pathetic it would be to sit in fancy restaurants and listen to him ramble on if only to puke up pricey wine of an evening. No. There's more than that. Of course there is.

You could at least pretend to be interested, he says.

No, I couldn't, she replies, sneering, and he laughs, he thinks its all a game, thinks this is some harsh little roleplay they have. But it isn't. She hates every last single thing about him, has hated him since the first day they met.

It was 4am at a blurry bar. She was dressed as a zombie. A bride undead, to be precise, and so drunk that her eyes rolled back in her head, lending her costume an uncanny resemblance to its inspiration. He bought everyone champagne and she noticed he was there; made no choice to go, but ended up in his car, found herself in his bed. She had given up on men; none would give her what she wanted, and neither would women, so she embraced ambivalence, being taken if she was taken, staying celibate if she was not. And, it appeared, that night she was going to be had.

It all changed in an instant. He picked her up, over-the-threshold style, to ease the duty of her tequila knees, and laid her out on crisp white Egyptian cotton, the soles of her feet taking in an uninterrupted view of the sunrise over the ocean. She was almost impressed, and told him so, and he slapped her, and that was the moment. She came alive with blood rushing straight to her face; became swollen with the very feeling of it. Finally, it was all made real.

She bit him on the mouth, hard, to bring blood. He pulled his face back; she wouldn't let go, wouldn't stop, 'til she could taste the metal of it run onto her gums and finally, blessedly, she felt the unencumbered punch.

He immediately pleaded, apologized, removed himself from the bed. Her head snapped to the side. She tongued the tooth that had come loose, as she'd always dreamed of, and felt herself flood. A demonic grin, she knew, but couldn't help it, she looked towards him and said, simply: *Again.*

And now, addicted. It happens. When one dealer holds the only stash, his business is guaranteed. A single provider. Monopoly on her pleasure. He had it, the bastard, and she hated him for that. Hated every single moment she had to spend with him, waiting for what she wanted.

Finish your wine, he says.

Fuck yourself, she says. He won't respond until they're out of the door.

Outside. Woozy. A car pulls up. She sits herself on the cab seat, ass first, knees out of the car, and sits there long enough for him to comment on how long it's taking her to get in. Half way through the rebuke she tugs her skirt up higher, closes her eyes, parts her knees. When none of the strangers on the street pay attention, she takes a finger and reaches around, down and under, passing lace, into the wetness. She moans. Then louder. Heads turn towards the car, and her hanging out of it, knuckle deep inside herself. A young male voice yelps. Others join in. All male, all of them cheering.

Don't be such a fucking whore, he says, and she feels it, that first thrust. A fission of sorts; the two feelings becoming. Hate turning into two. Hate and. Something else. He slaps her legs into the cab and she purrs, calls him a cunt, and when he doesn't rise to it it's all okay, because she knows he will, he'll get riled and angry, it's always only a matter of time.

You're a fucking embarrassment, he says, because he knows that she likes it, and he likes her, and he likes the game, though he doesn't know really that he's the only one playing.

If there's anything about this that pains her, it's that they all see his fingers tighten round her throat, but none of them see that she holds her neck out, strong and regal, and he brings his hand up to it. A hand that she has made turgid with rage, a hand that she has taught. None of them see him come to her; they all assume it's the other way around.

But no matter, she thinks, or rather doesn't think, as the cracks of knuckle on cheek bone grow more rapid, and the warmth of his spit gently rolls down her face, and, finally, as the space in her chest convulses, pleading, his hand over her mouth, his fingers pinching her nose closed, and too long, it's just that little bit too long, and her lungs are screaming and it's all white noise and finally, finally, the thoughts fall away.

A dull thump back to Earth. The gasp of breath. She clings to the warmth of oblivion but it cools. He pushes himself into her, and she says, simply: *Again*.

FUCK THE NIGHT

LUCY HOLDEN

I am the sooty underside
of a bat's wing.
I am the dreaded
in the darkness.
I am the act of regretting
doing--
and failing.
At times like these,
I am everything
that was ever nothing.

I am black skinny jeans
eyeliner and lipstick.
I am a slogan devoid of permanence
written in a moment
for a moment.
I am an attack
without follow through,
heavy on sharp objects
but small on manpower.
On days like these,
I am the underside
of nightfall.

I am cities and alleys
Curses and streets
I am arching over doorways
I stir past the edge of sight.

I am the silence
that follows silence
in the leaden moment
of waking into a dream.
I am a throwing stone
I am the gravel under sleet
I am a stained sheet,
discarded, burned,
burned.

I am the screen of a dead computer
I am the screams of the living
I am the dirt in the ground of your grave
I am the patch of space
where a star once burned
Now the black hole sucks up its surroundings
-craving an ending-
in a world without end,
amen

I SUPPOSE, IN THE END, WE ARE ALL SEARCHING FOR SOMETHING...

FLIM FLAM

SCRIPT: PAUL BRISTOW
ARTWORK: MHAIRI ROBERTSON

... AND I FOUND IT ON A STANDARD CULTURE DROP. A QUICK STOP OFF ON AN ALREADY SURVEYED PLANET TO OBSERVE AND RECORD LOCAL LIFE FORMS PRIOR TO PLANETARY ASSET STRIPPING.

THE PLANET HAD NO SENTIENT LIFE REGISTERED, SO IT TOOK ME A MOMENT OR TWO TO UNDERSTAND WHAT I WAS HEARING.

THE PLATITUDEYPUS IS NOT PRETTY. IT DOES NOT MAKE USEFUL HATS OR MITTENS. IT TASTES FOUL. BUT IT HAS ONE UNIQUE SKILL.

it was meant to be

BY GENETIC FLUKE, ITS MATING CALLS SOUND EXACTLY LIKE THE HALF-BAKED WISDOM PEOPLE LIKE TO HEAR IN TIMES OF PERSONAL CRISIS.

A MALE PLATITUDEYPUS COULD BE SIGNALLING ALL FEMALES WITHIN A FIVE MILE RADIUS, AND TO OUR EARS, IT WOULD SOUND LIKE ...

happiness is just sadness spelled differently

THE FACT THAT THIS FLIMSY JIBBERISH IS ULTIMATELY USELESS IS NEITHER HERE NOR THERE. AFTER ALL ...

BrioISHHzzz

... WHO WANTS PRACTICAL SOLUTIONS OR MISERABLE RATIONALISM WHEN YOU CAN LISTEN TO A REASSURING PLATITUDEYPUS INSTEAD?

I KNEW IMMEDIATELY THAT I WAS GOING TO BE VERY RICH.

I TOOK HALF A DOZEN ONTO THE CRAFT TO BEGIN WITH. THERE WAS NO FUSS. THEY SEEMED DOCILE ENOUGH. BUT VOCAL.

SWIFTLY EDITED RECORDINGS FROM THIS FIRST GROUP WERE RELEASED AS AN AUDIOBOOK ON INCREASING SELF-ESTEEM THROUGH INTERPRETIVE DANCE.

IT WAS A BEST SELLING HIT BEFORE I EVEN LEFT THE PLANET.

HERDS OR FAMILIES OF CAPTIVE PLATITUDCYPI LEARNED QUICKLY TO SYNCHRONISE THE STYLE AND THEME OF THEIR MATING CALLS...

... ENSURING THAT WITHIN DAYS YOU WOULD HAVE ENOUGH MATERIAL FOR A BOOK ON MANAGEMENT THEORY OR THE POWER OF POSITIVE THINKING.

AND ALL YOU NEEDED WAS SOME CAGES.

FOR A WHILE, EVERYTHING WAS PERFECT. I CORNERED THE MARKET ON SELF-SERVING SELF HELP.

EVEN BETTER, GANGS OF ANGRY RATIONALISTS, INCENSED BY THE POPULARITY OF SUCH PATENTLY RIDICULOUS ADVICE...

... BEGAN A CAMPAIGN OF BRUTAL FUNDAMENTALISM, CULLING THE BEAST WHEREVER POSSIBLE. THE SCARCITY INCREASED THEIR VALUE IMMENSELY.

GLORY DAYS.

THEN...
IT ALL STARTED TO WRONG.

FEELINGS ARE GOOD!!

CONSIDER EACH FLOWER ANEW!!

PEOPLE, COMMUNITIES, WHOLE COUNTRIES, ALL BEGAN INTERPRETING THE MESSAGES IN WILDLY OPPOSING WAYS. SELF-ACTUALISATION WARS BROKE OUT ACROSS THE GALAXY.

IN THE COLD DEVASTATION THAT FOLLOWED, EVERYONE JUST NEEDED SOMETHING TO BELIEVE IN AGAIN.

THE HARDY PLATITUDEYPUS HAD WEATHERED THE WAR WELL.
STILL HERE.
STILL SAYING WHATEVER PEOPLE NEEDED TO HEAR.

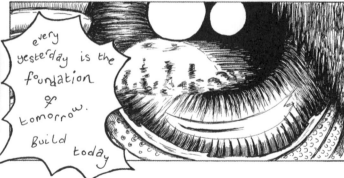

every yesterday is the foundation of tomorrow. build today

WE ARE ALL SEARCHING FOR SOMETHING. LOOKING FOR MEANING AND TRYING TO SURVIVE IN A COLD COSMOS. BUT THEN, SO IS EVERYONE ELSE.

IN MY ARROGANCE, I HAVE MISUNDERSTOOD THE BIOLOGICAL IMPERATIVE OF THE PLATITUDEYPUS.

AND CREATED THE OPPORTUNITY FOR OUR OWN EXTINCTION.

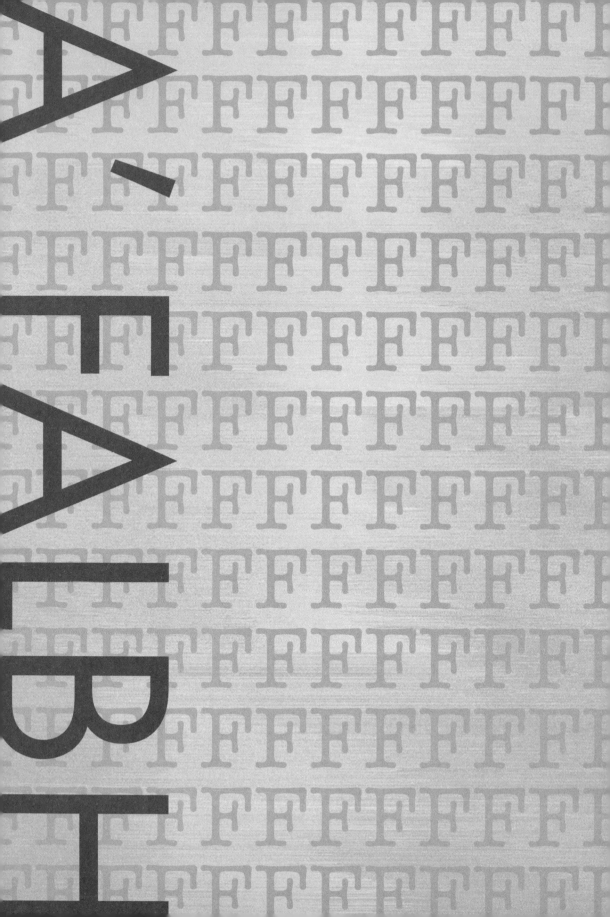

A' FALBH

COLM MACQUEEN

'S ann ann an cridhe na h-Eòrpa a thòisich an cianalas.
Cha bhith mi tuilleadh nam thràill dhan ghnìomhachas.
An t-àm son seann dhùthaich ùr. Dreuchd ùr. Beatha ùr.

Litir a-staigh gu puncail.
Glainneachan fìon le co-obraichean,
Faclan còir, càirt snog.
Jammer dat je weggaat! 'S truagh gu bheil thu a' falbh.
Tapadh leibh. Bha e math a bhith còmhla ribh.
Slàn leibh.

12 Sràid na h-Òigh, Bruiseal.
An ceathramh latha air fhichead dhen Fhaoilleach, dà mhìle 's a trì deug
Aig dà uair sa mhadainn: am flat sgiobalta
Aig trì uairean sa mhadainn: na pocannan 's bogsaichean seulaichte, làn
Aig deich uairean sa mhadainn: an làr glan.

Air beulaibh an taighe, co-ogha charaid m' athair
deiseil le bhana falamh.
Poca air phoca,
bogsa air bhogsa,
màileid air mhàileid.
Air beulaibh an taighe, co-ogha charaid m' athair
deiseil le bhana làn, an dorus fosgailte.

An dorus dùinte.
Air ais leis an iuchair,
air ais dhan uachdaran.
Merci Monsieur.

Dag België!
Tschüß Belgien!
Au revoir la Belgique!
Au revoir la Belgique?
Chun an ath thuras?
Uill, tìoraidh an dràsta co-dhiù.

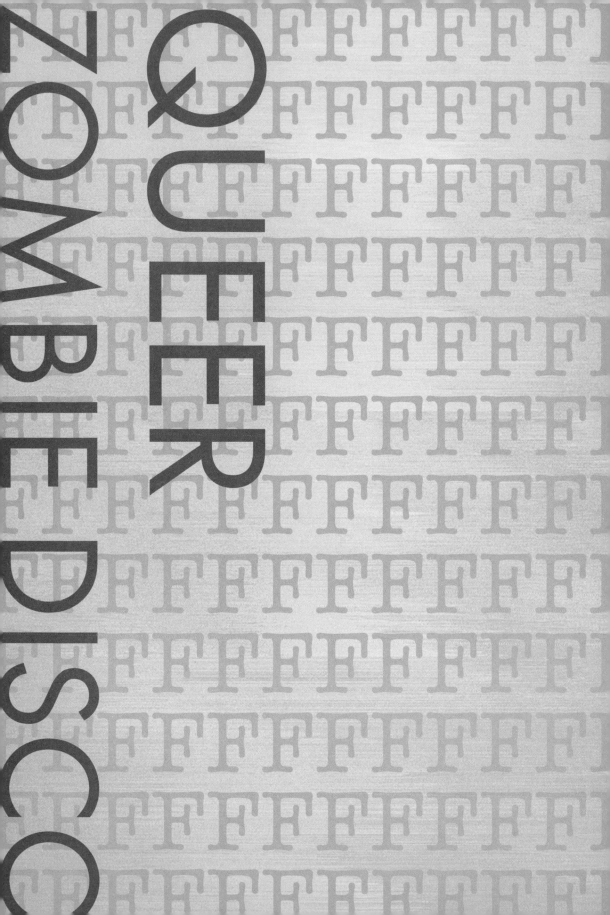

QUEER ZOMBIE DISCO

KIRSTY LOGAN

#1: I love you more than I love to eat brains

After the show Mara coils her intestines up carefully and threads them back through the hemmed slit of her bellybutton. I mirror her, coiling up her guitar leads and putting them behind the amps so she doesn't get them mixed up. She did that once before and the electric shock fried part of her liver – we had to eat three boys to get that back.

Tukie's busy with the drums, unscrewing the high-hats cos she'll be getting drunk and smashing them round people's head at the afterparty. She lost most of her fingertips the last time she did that, so maybe she won't bust so many eyeballs this time round. That was fucking messy. Plus the crowd tonight was mostly hotbloods, it looked like – though they'd have to be dumb to come to the afterparty cos there's no security there – and they don't smash so good. Tukie'll get bored of them pretty quick and we can all get back to pouring shots into her bone marrow like we used to.

Mara's done with her guts so she comes over to help me with the leads – I'm having some trouble cos my scapula's bent funny. Last week we ate a bunch of drunk hotblood girls, it grew Mara's clitoral hood back, and now she wants me to fuck her really hard all the time. I invited this punk kid with a blonde and pink mohawk to the afterparty; I could see through a rip in his shoulder that he still had a whole clavicle, so he should fix that.

I have great peripheral vision just now cos I'm missing my left temple, so I can see the look Mara's giving me – even with a bit of her jaw missing she can do that fuckable smirk. I wind the leads slowly, my messed-up scapula clicking with every twist.

Tukie's got the high-hats unscrewed and she's practicing her smash-action on the bigtitted babydyke sound tech, who's giggling and feeding Tukie the falling shreds of earlobe and eyelid, so I figure it's a good time for me and Mara to disappear. I twirl the guitar lead and lasso her in for a kiss. Jawbones scrape, dry tongues rasp; she presses her sternum against my nipple, and I'm gone.

#2: All they have to lose is their graves; all we have to lose is our brains

I feel like shit and like nothing at the same time. The feeling-shit part is mostly just memory – knowing how I would have felt if I still had brain cells to dehydrate or a liver to poison. The knowledge that it can't really hurt isn't as strong as the memory that it should. The part of my brain that remembers those hotblood hangovers knows what it needs: water, painkillers, a fry-up. I wander round the flat, trying to find a working tap and taking stock of the debris from the night. It's not my flat so I don't really give a shit, but it looks pretty fucked-up. There are handprints and footprints and random smeared bodypart-prints all over the walls. Something dark is dripping from the ceiling. Shreds of toe and scalp – the unappetising bits – are piled up on the windowsills. Bodies are curled up together after the best or worst or most indifferent night of their lives. Everything smells of dust and flesh. To be honest, the place could all have looked like that before last night.

Tukie's crashed out on the floor, limbs tangled around the bigtitted babydyke sound tech. It's not obvious whose limbs are whose or even if they're attached to either of them, but it doesn't really matter. Our tour is moving on to the next town today, so there'll be some new dumbfuck hotbloods for us to chow down on. Besides, we could use a sound tech. I dig my toe into Tukie's side until she starts twitching, then leave her to wake up. She keeps the keys for the van wedged between her collarbones, so we can't go without her.

I can't find a tap that works, but I manage to suck up some liquid from the broken end of a water pipe in the kitchen. It mostly falls right out again, pooling around my feet and soaking into the fabric of my Converse. I hate the feeling of having wet feet, so I rub them dry with a hank of blonde hair I think I remember yanking from someone's head and abandoning in the bathroom sink.

I finally find Mara, mostly in one piece, but with someone's ankle bone imbedded in her temple. I take that as a sign that it's time to go. I hoist Mara up onto my shoulder, climb over the slow-breathing bodies in the doorway, and prop her up in the backseat. I work on digging the ankle bone out of her skull until Tukie and the babydyke stagger out and start up the van.

#3. Don't eat the brains from my head; let's just make out instead

Five minutes before we're meant to be on stage, and Mara wants to fuck. We're both missing our perinea so it's a bit messy, but last week I crushed my hands under an amp and Mara's going crazy for the way I fuck her with all my fingers triple-jointed. We barricade ourselves in the only toilet cubicle with a lock that works, and bury ourselves in each other. Her cunt smells of wet earth and fresh blood, and when she comes she screams so hard her tongue splits. She sits me up on the tank and shows me how a split tongue feels – I can't describe it, but I can say it sent my feet into spasms. When we open the door, none of the cubicles have working locks.

Backstage, Tukie is still making out with the sound tech. They're both missing all their extremities cos they like to feed each other fingertips and earlobes as a romantic gesture, a reminder of their first meeting. It's been months and they're still at it, though they have to eat a dozen hotbloods a week just to grow everything back. Still, there are plenty more where they came from.

Tukie stops nibbling on the sound tech and starts wiping the gore off her high-hats. Mara winks at me – she has both her eyelids at the moment so it looks hot as fuck – and goes off to find her mic stand. I sling on my guitar and load up my pockets with plectrums.

We've changed around the setlist tonight, making sure our final song is a noisy one so that everyone in the bar upstairs will think all the noise is just us playing, rather than the crowd. We've already wedged the van up against the fire doors, so we don't need to worry about them getting out that way. I'm pretty sure tonight will be a messy one, and we won't be able to come back here again. But that's okay. Next week we're coming to your town.

THE FUTURE

THE FUTURE

CHRIS BOYLAND

The future is a 'two for one' deal when you
can't afford to pay for one. It's a discount card
for a store where you can get 30% off as long
as you spend more money than you can afford.
The future is an opportunity to consume the same
products you consume today, repackaged with
a new logo, and a heart-warming message from
an anime goldfish.

The future will let you be special in the same
way as everyone else is special and to stand out
by fitting in. You won't dress differently, in the
future, but you will feel different about the way
you dress. There will be more youth cults for old
people, to deconstruct and de-contextualise and
remind us all that things were always better in the
old days.

In the future, facts will be rendered obsolete
and your opinions will be substantiated by the
number of 'likes' you are able to gather on social
media. Decisions about the future will be made,
based on the views of "so-called experts", weighted
according to the brand of soft drink they promote
and their ability to succeed in a series of televised,
dance-off competitions.

The future will provide an ironic commentary
on the future, as it happens, spooled out over
screens and streams and social-media feeds.

It will be re-mixed, re-formatted and re-imagined
in real-time, while a nation 'Ooh's and 'Aah's over
the latest display of interactive, artisan baked goods,
cooked up on a conveyor belt, in a factory, in
Shenzen.

In the future, everyone will have a safe space,
and everyone will be confined to their safe space,
during curfew hours, this will be for your comfort
and protection, to ensure that, in the future, no-one
has to rub up against a dissenting voice or opinion,
which might otherwise challenge your deeply held
belief, that no-one understands you quite like you do.

The future is an opportunity to opportunistically
re-frame your idea of the future, according to
whatever personal beliefs or ambitions you may
hold, and then to blame other people when, for
some mysterious reason, your vision of the future
fails to come true.

In the future, your voice will be a small voice,
assembled from found words in forgotten places
and broadcast over a dead channel and it will be
screaming, "Wake up, Wake up, Wake up!
WAKE UP!".

THE CURIOUS CASE

OF THE

F-WORD MACHINE

THE CURIOUS CASE OF THE F-WORD MACHINE

JEFFREY G. ROBERTS

Fortnoy Futznagel was an uncommon man. Uncommonly common. A skinny little troll of a specimen; in the dictionary under 'door mat', it said: 'see Fortnoy Futznagel.'

Now, everyone has to have a purpose in life – a need to wake up each morning to do – something. *His* was like a red hot poker in the pit of his stomach. And it was called 'revenge'. Against who? Why, everyone, of course! Well, almost everyone. From the bullies who tormented him in high school, to his control freak bosses when he entered the work force, to the girls who delighted in egging him on with their charms, then ran away laughing.

Ah, but Fortnoy Futznagel had an ace up his sleeve others did not; a way to level the playing field – and then go above and beyond it. You see, he had an I.Q. of 195. But you've heard the old adage: that there's a thin dividing line between genius and insanity? Well, Futznagel was erasing it. From his plan to turn gold into lead, so that the world might never run out of pencils; to building a hand-held fan that sported fan blades at both ends, spinning in opposite directions. The result: the cancellation of *any* breeze. For what purpose? *Why, for people who thought the air temperature was perfect just the way it was*, Futznagel would proudly proclaim!

But his pride and joy? His crowning achievement? The one bizarre device which – he was convinced – would not only grant him a hallowed place in the pantheon of all the scientific geniuses who had come before him – it was also his surefire way to amass immense wealth. And with that wealth, he would right some wrongs, teach some lessons to certain people who desperately needed it; and, if he could shame some of those high school girls to tears, in public? Well, that would be the icing on the cake to him!

But what kind of machine could achieve such disparate objectives? He revealed little of his design, and to few people. (Well, the baker down the street. Fortnoy Futznagel believed doughnuts were next to Godliness, and the closest thing on Earth to Heaven. It mattered little that his baker friend thought Futznagel to be beyond bonkers.) But he told him one night anyway, just before the bakery closed. His friend listened intently; partly out of morbid curiosity, and partly out of fear of what loony Futznagel might do to him, if mocked. Fortnoy looked left. He looked right, making sure all the remaining bakery customers had now left.

'It's my F-Word Machine, Charlie!'

'I beg your pardon, Fortnoy?' He quietly fingered a rolling pin behind him, just in case Futznagel went psycho, and he'd have to clobber him into submission. 'And why do you keep looking over your shoulder? There's nobody here but you and I. Unless you think my cupcakes are planning on creaming you.' And he laughed at his own joke. Fortnoy wasn't laughing.

'I wouldn't be too sure. Anything's possible, Charlie.'

'Like I said – I beg your pardon?'

'My machine,' he continued, darting his eyes left and right, 'I believe is developing consciousness. Like the American Indian belief in the Manitou – the life force in everything.'

Charlie the baker found himself shooting a glance at his freshly baked cupcakes, then shook the silly thought out of his head.

'I wouldn't be surprised if that life force followed me here, and even now is plotting with the meringue!' He was getting truly paranoid.

'Uh – okay, Fortnoy,' he said slowly. 'Why don't you sit down, have a cup of coffee with me, and tell me all about this F-Word Machine.' Maybe talking, and a quiet cup of coffee with someone he trusted, would calm him down, Charlie thought.

'Well, I built it in my basement, after studying the mathematics of probability. I reasoned that I could build a kind of printing press, with a number of motorized discs on a long shaft – much like the old style automobile odometers. Each disc would have mostly the letter 'F' imprinted on it, since I've determined that's the most utilized letter in the English language, (and it's my name). Plus the numbers 0-9 – except the last two discs, which would have all 26 letters of the alphabet on them. The machine would continuously print, at random, line after line of impressions from the discs, onto a giant roll of paper fed through it. Eventually it would print everything ever said or written , or which *will* be said or written! Ordinarily this would take millions of years (and I haven't enough vitamins to last that long). But by reducing the number of discs with the *entire* alphabet to just two, plus a special algorithm I've devised, I believe I've significantly reduced that time by a factor of 25. Eventually, I'll learn of the wonders to come for the next hundred centuries! Think of the discoveries I'll have access to, and knowledge of! I'll be the richest man on Earth! And then I can start to set things straight – all thanks to the Futznagel F-Word Machine!'

'I see,' Charlie said, not really seeing.

'But I think it's developing a mind of its own! I don't think it likes me!'

'Astute machine,' Charlie thought.

'For the first few weeks the discs printed out only nonsense on the paper: BUNNY DUST, BOOJA KLEIN THUMB SNOT, PENILE PROPELLOR PUS – things like that. But I know it's imminent! Any day it will print a major discovery!' He couldn't sit still, and started fidgeting. Apparently the coffee only made him more wired, and his eyes began darting all around him; as if he expected something to wreak vengeance upon him at any moment. 'It was a mistake to come here. But I was hungry!' He took his two dozen doughnuts, and hastily left. Charlie watched him as he walked quickly down the street, constantly looking left, right, and behind him. Fortnoy was convinced his machine was out to get him. But the lure of impending wealth and revenge was a drug he could not, would not forsake. He never left his basement after that.

He hadn't slept in days. And he brought a cot to the basement so he could always keep tabs on the constantly running machine. Literally, he slept with one eye open; partly waiting to see his F-Word Machine print out all the scientific discoveries of 2375 – and partly out of fear the machine would kill him while he slept. He looked like hell. In his paranoia he imagined the contraption begin to look like a face. An accusatory face. And it wasn't hard to imagine in his state of mind: giant brass gears constantly turning looked like glowering eyes; wires and cables everywhere he imagined were morphing into deadly tentacles. And the sound it made. Oh, that sound! Was that whisperings he heard amongst the turning gears? Every few hours he'd wake up to check out what it had printed. But all he read were things like: SPOOKY TOOTH LAS VEGAS and PUMPKIN FARTS FOR MARS. He was getting angry. And even more paranoid.

Until one night, at precisely 1:23 AM, he spied his F-Word Machine beginning to print out something… intriguing. He jumped up, wiping the sleep from his eyes, donned his thick beer bottle glasses, and intently began to read what was on the roll, among the thousands of crumpled up sheets cluttering the floor. It said: 2126. KEY INGRED…FOR X-RAY VISI…FOUND TO BE FO… And that is all it said. Nothing more.

'FO! FO what? What's the rest of it, you stupid machine!? Can't you even print out a whole sentence!? You think I'm doing this for my health? For fun?' And in a fit of rage he picked up a glass and threw it at the machine. It shattered, but did not damage it.

'Ouch!' the machine said silently to itself.

Two nights later, while going over his detailed plans for world conquest – once his machine provided him with the knowledge to do so – he saw, out of the corner of his eye, the machine printing a word that got his attention. Rushing up to it, he saw the discs and cogs still printing out line after line of gibberish. And then there was this: 2033. PANCAKE SYRUP DISCOV…CURE FOR FI…

'What!? What!? A cure for some horrible disease I could be filthy rich from – and that's all you can say! How stupid can you be! Moronic contraption!' And he kicked it.

'Ee-yoww!' the machine said to itself, wincing in pain.

Futznagel decided to cover it up, but allowed it to keep running continuously. Thus, he could get some sleep, and in a week he'd uncover it, and surely find printed, some magnificent invention from the 25th century. Power and riches would be his!

A week later, he eagerly uncovered it. By now, his basement was knee deep with hundreds of yards of six-foot wide reams of paper, all imprinted with unintelligible nonsense such as: TURPENTINE HOO-HA BOOBS and DAD'S TURKEY CARBURETTOR. But then he spotted it. One line, which said: 2124. 50 TRILLION DOLLA…AMASS USING 6 CORN FLAKE…

Futznagel thought the top of his head would fly off. 'You brass and plastic imbecile! I didn't build you to spit out piecemeal answers to world problems! How am I supposed to amass fame and fortune from a stuttering pile of brass crap like you?' And he threw a week old pizza at it, as hard as he could.

'Owww! Damn it!' the F-Word Machine responded to itself.

He was so mad he was ready to dismantle it. He felt it was mocking him. But he'd give it the benefit of the doubt – and try one more time.

Three nights later he had his chance. At 4:00 AM the sound of whirring gears printing something woke him up. He put on his glasses, stumbled out of his makeshift bed, and eagerly peered down at the paper coming out from the wheels. It said: 2094. 8000 GIRLS THROW THEM…LUST AT 1 MAN WHO DISCOVERS FY…

That did it. He could take no more. He was beyond enraged. He picked up an axe, to finally destroy his F-Word Machine, and relegate the pieces to the dumpster – where they belonged! No product of his own genius was going to make a fool out of him!

A month later, an odd smell began wafting out of his basement. Neighbours became alarmed – and contacted the authorities. What they found in Fortnoy Futznagel's basement wasn't a pretty sight. There was his decomposing body on the floor, with a large brass gear neatly embedded in his head. Somehow, without anyone hearing it, his contraption had exploded. But there, lying amidst the rubble, was a wide strip of paper with gibberish printed on it. Except for one complete and perfectly understandable line – FUCK YOU, FORTNOY FUTZNAGEL!

TALK TO FRANK

We chat to Frank Iero about his favourte fiction and films.
Don't say you're not getting your money's worth of F-words.

Frank Iero is a man of many musical talents. He's worn his influences on his sleeve through the last decade and a half in My Chemical Romance, Death Spells, and the various incarnations of his own band, the Patience. He lives and breathes music. But in the spirit of the F-Word, we opted to dive into his fiction and film loves.

The natural place to start, then, is what he's reading at the moment. 'I'm currently reading *The Bob Dylan Chronicle*, book one. And, actually, I recently started *The Master and Margarita* [Mikhail Bulgakov]. I guess, usually, the specific topics will grab my interest so that I pick up a book, but with *The Master and Margarita*, we were just over in Russia, and we toured there for about three weeks and I was actually given multiple copies of it because the author was from there and they were proud of it, and just wanted me to read it.

'So far, it's basically about the devil coming in... Basically it's the premise of 'Sympathy for the Devil' where they got their idea for the song. The devil comes in and steers people in certain ways and makes these deals. That's just the start. I've recently started it so I'm not even very far in! Pretty interesting so far.'

It comes as no surprise to those who have followed Frank's blood-splattered music career to discover that his preferences have always leaned towards horror. Stephen King comes up a lot.

And through his teens he found himself drawn to others like Ray Bradbury, Kurt Vonnegut and J.D. Salinger.

He's given the impossible task as a reader: your definitive, top five books. He gets four tomes in and suddenly every book that he loves comes flying at him. 'Oh and, man, I can't pick!'

'Okay', we say, he can have one extra. 'It has to be a tie between...' He thinks a bit more, and *Fear and Loathing in Las Vegas* and *American Psycho* make the cut.

'I love how vivid they are,' he gushes, on what makes his favourites exactly that. 'You really get transported when you read those books. All the authors, I think, of those books collectively, they have such a descriptive way of talking. They really push you.'

'Alright, so, *American Psycho*, right? You feel dirty reading that book,' he laughs. 'I feel like that book above any other really, really makes you delve into some topics that no book would normally. Even, like, J.D. Salinger, his speech in *Catcher in the Rye* is so much different to that in *Franny and Zooey*. The characters interact, they really feel alive, and that's what's so captivating about a great author.'

FRANK'S TOP BOOKS

Fear and Loathing in Las Vegas – Hunter S Thompson
American Psycho – Brett Easton Ellis
Slaughterhouse-Five – Kurt Vonnegut
The Shining – Stephen King
The Book Thief – Markus Zusak
Franny and Zooey – J.D. Salinger

Photo: Sinead Grainger

When it comes to film, Frank talks about who he watched them with as much, if not more, than the films themselves. It seems a common theme that regardless of genre, age or location, what makes films stand out is largely indebted to how he came to see it.

'I watched *Under The Skin* recently – that movie was just mesmerizing for me. I feel like that movie was very polarising for people. My wife hated it! I remember I was just totally captivated by it.

'Growing up, I was very much into the horror genre. That was one of the things that my father and I really were able to bond over. There was stuff from his youth, like old Universal and things of that nature, I remember going to see as a kid at the theatre. I remember being pretty young and him showing me *House on the Haunted Hill* and *The Thing* movies and all these

sorts of films. That was just always my go-to genre.'

He took a lot from his father in terms of culture, and as a father himself, Frank does admit that there's a lot in the literary and movie tank he's ready to pass down. But with the likes of Stephen King topping his lists, it'll likely be a few years before he can make a start...

'Aw, man. It's hard because they're so young. I'm still kind of finding that fine line of what they can really understand but definitely so much to share with them. I think one of the greatest things about my kids is that they truly love reading. They started reading very early on and really enjoy me just sitting down with a book and reading a story, so we do stories every night. And we're getting into chapter books and stuff, but it's very much like *The Dolphin*

School or very young reader type thing, over King,' he laughs.

'We actually started reading *Harry Potter* which they're really into, and I definitely have a bookcase full of stuff that I hope they get into at some point. But right now, I look at a lot and think "I don't know if this is appropriate!"'

Turns out, *Harry Potter* is, in its own way, a series he is passing down. It was the way in which he passed many an hour on the road with My Chemical Romance back in the day.

'I loved it! You know, I read them all on tour. I started reading them maybe around [*Harry Potter and the*] *Half Blood Prince*. When *Half Blood Prince* came out, I went in on them all. J. K. Rowling is incredibly captivating as an author and storyteller. Plus, as a young person: who doesn't want to have that? The idea that you wake up one day and find out that everything that you knew is wrong and the inkling that you had that there was something spectacular out there is true – I feel like that's a common fantasy for kids, y'know? And for adults. I think that's why people are so apt to want to believe in God.'

Frank Iero took on the challenge of filtering a lifetime of reading and viewing into two small lists, and on top of getting a few extra, he spoke at length and excitedly about them, something he really loves to do but doesn't often get the chance. So, if you're ever looking for a conversation starter with Frank, there you go.

FRANK'S TOP FILMS

'Let's see,' he begins. 'Well, definitely…' he pauses. 'Aw, man. This is hard!'

'*Die Hard* is up there. Absolutely.
Taxi Driver.
Uhhh. Jeez.
Interstellar is up there.
I just rewatched *Donnie Darko* the other night and I thought that was so good. It's still one of my favourites. I think it's absolutely phenomenal.
Brazil, I love.
All the old Scorcese stuff.

'I lost count of where I am!' The only way to solve the predicament is to go a wander through his house to find films on his shelves.

'*Ghostbusters I* and *II* basically. Here's the thing that's really fun – on tour, there's this book of movies that we bring with us all over, and *Ghostbusters* is always in there.

'*Home Alone* is always in there! And I could probably go through the entire movie and say it line for line. It's kind of hilarious. And that kind of thing goes back to my youth of seeing that movie.

'I'd like to give you one more to end on: *Dawn of the Dead*.'

Nice.

53

THE MATCH

THE MATCH

STEVIE MCEWAN

9-0-6-5-1

I put the ticket back in my pocket, and sat down.

For three hours I'd queued outside. And we knew that being made to wait was deliberate, the club hated the raffle being more popular than the match. Aye, even this match. *THE WORLD'S GREATEST DERBY!* the screens reminded us. *1 BILLION VIEWERS!* It was mad, this skint, bedraggled crowd turning up for just a half-time draw. And I thought I had no chance. I'd never even been close before. As people would jump screaming from their seats, I'd sink further into mine.

But you never know, do you?

Ten minutes until kick-off, and the screen (sponsor – CK Oxygen) commanded ON YOUR FEET! I took my green and white scarf and I stood. *Be Proud!* the screen declared. *Be Loud!* And the words spilled out for us all to sing. The state of it. Dangling out of reach our soul that they stole, and now selling it back to us alien and bloated. But I still sang of course. My scarf above like a sign reading SOLD.

The thousands opposite responded with jeers. Then on a command of their own, a sea emerged of blue, white and red. They sang. We booed. We sang. They booed. I gazed about. From some rows in front there was a *fucking up yeez!* It caused a ripple of laughs. A wee clap. But no. It was a bad move.

Five minutes to go. There'd be forty-five after that, and injury time. But this was nothing compared to the months I'd waited, and feeling an ever-deepening nausea I took a breath. Was I ready for this? If I won, could I *handle* the prize? There were mutters and glances, and I strained ahead for a look. Our swearer was gone. The club brags about its *Criminal Response Time* like it's some fastest goal award, and no wonder, that kicking out took seconds. He was lucky in a way. He'd miss the match. But he'd miss the draw as well.

9-0-6-5-1

The teams ran out. The digital puppeteers worked our hands, feet and mouths, and the stadium ignited. Then, kick-off. There'd been a time when you'd forget yourself and linger off your seat for a bit. But not these days. I stretched out my legs. There were four players who'd joined last week and would be gone in the morning. A Chinese guy representing a sponsor. A banker who'd paid a mint just to play this match.

A goal was on its way. The screen knew it, spewing its extravaganza of glittery green and gold (sponsor – Barton's Blood). And when we scored, I *felt* something. A tiny, latent thrill that helped me off my seat. It wasn't just me. We all got it. After everything we've been through, this club is still *in* us. But when I sat back down, the remote trace of joy was wiped away by hundreds grabbing at their mics. Not me. There's only so much I can take. As the scorer stopped at the camera and grinned, I didn't get ready. As he held up some fingers, I stared at the floor. Then he started gesturing. He moved and he signaled, and loads of fans shouted their guesses. Chocolates. Oxygen. Cars. Some shouted for so long I was sure they were reading from a list. Some screamed so loudly I knew their kids were starving. One guessed the right product, and he went to collect his prize. It was big. But nothing compared to what would come.

The match restarted. We scored again. They scored too. And us again. The stopping and starting was bugging me now, and for a moment I wished I'd stayed home. With a minute left most of us were no longer watching. We were staring at our tickets. Muttering at the sky. Then came the whistle and a roof-raising roar. The billion viewers would have no idea. No clue that this bedlam was not for what had happened but what *would*. The cameras paused and TV companies broke off. The world had gone.

The draw started with the away fans. Their first winner was met with a cheer, and from their tiny whirls of chaos, illegal flags emerged. But then we couldn't hear. We could barely hear ourselves. Choruses stamped the air. Banners screamed out slogans. We surfed on waves of songs as finally the day had *started*. In our seething mass a guy was taking off his jeans. Another was emptying his pockets. A woman was peeling off her shoes. One more was touching her toes. Deals were made to borrow all the right gear. But I'd wait until I'd won.

Finally it was us, and again I checked.

9-0-6-5-1

The first number drew a scream, a guy with a big belly plunged down the steps and onto the trackside. Next, a skinny girl raced down the aisle and vaulted onto the pitch. Then a tall guy jogged on, he waved and kissed the ground. A gaunt looking boy then entered, holding his stomach like this might stop him throwing up. Out kept coming the numbers. On kept coming the fans. Until, of the eleven places, only one was left.

9!

0!

6!

5!

7!

I fell onto my seat. Next time maybe.

I got back up. I screamed out my support for the ginger-haired guy striding down the aisle, and when he hit the pitch with a cartwheel I knew his playing would be for the best. Our line-up looked strong, I thought. Then again, so did theirs. Aye, whatever would happen, these twelve minutes would be a cracker. I roared at the eleven dreams that had now come true. And then, before the inevitable return of the impostors, I watched the World's Greatest Derby.

NOTICE

NOT NICE

NOT NICE

HELEN VICTORIA MURRAY

I have been practising the art of redaction.
I cut seventeen lines from the heart of this poem
So that it would align with my personal thesis

Of the great grand readerly acceptable.
Imagine what profanity preceded

This,
then.
That:

I want to rewrite history
On your neck, with my teeth
Devise some invention, that you might:

Fuck me without ever kissing or touching me.
Fuck me under the table we sit at in my memory.
Fuck me enveloped in the ghost of the first night we met.

AN OPEN LETTER TO THE MEN THAT FRIGHTEN ME

AN OPEN LETTER TO THE MEN THAT FRIGHTEN ME

SUZEY INGOLD

This is an open letter to the men that frighten me.

It's not you, it's me.

That's a lie – it's you. It's you, the collective you, that have caused this seemingly irrational fear of those who define themselves as male.

It's you, the seventeen year old with the tie askew, five years my junior, who makes an elaborately lewd comment to his school friends about my legs. Such poetry could put Shakespeare to shame.

It's you, the three-piece-suit-and-tie businessman, at least ten years my senior, who keeps on with the firm belief that the more times he calls me *love* or *sweetheart*, the more likely it is that I'll bend over for him. The kind of man to whom tried and true experience has whispered its promise that seniority and money may grant him ownership of the bodies of the women of the world. Mind, wit, and soul may be checked at the door.

It's you, the neighbour who greets me for the first time, drunk and threatening. Later, he'll shove a Christmas card through my door and tell me not to be shy, to *come round and visit sometime.* As though the sounds of a door slam from below or heavy footfall on the shared stairwell are not enough to make my entire body tense.

It's you, the bartender who glances down my top and says *it's on the house* and makes it sound like a compliment when really it wasn't complimentary in any sense of the word.

It's you, the drunk man on the street corner in the early hours of the morning who asks for directions and thanks me for my time by putting his hands on my arse and shoving his tongue into my mouth. The man I have to stop from following me home by looping twice more around the block instead of going straight in.

It's you, the male manager, because when he gives instructions to his employees, he's *doing his job.* But when I do it, *she's a right bossy cow.* But don't worry, because he'll hug it better later.

It's you, the twenty-something under the pulsing lights who doesn't even get as far as *hello*, let alone *can I buy you a drink?* before his hand is under my top.

It's you, the boy who walks me home from something that would not constitute a date and says *why not?* instead of *that's okay* when I tell him he's not coming inside. The boy who insists he just wants to talk at the same time as I'm pushing his hand out from my underwear for the third time in as many minutes.

It's you, the one that complains about the amount of men wrongly accused of sexual assault, but won't acknowledge the number of people – women, men, or otherwise – assaulted every year whose attackers are never brought to justice. 6% falsely accused, they estimate. 99% of perpetrators walk free.

It's you, the builder/man at the bus stop/_____ [insert male of your choice] who catcalls from across the street. From *hi, babe* to *fine, bitch* in half a minute.

It's me, for becoming so immune to it that I don't fight back.

It's me, for taking it as normal social standing.

See a group of men.

1. Look away.
2. Take a breath.
3. Speed up.
4. Hope for the best.

It's me, for the extensive map of NSFD (Not Safe For Dark) routes and their relatively risk-free counterparts that I have memorised, accompanied always by the *text me when you get home, yeah?*'s between girlfriends.

For the entire roadside safety manual of being a girl today that I was never taught but was forced to learn.

Not too low.

Not too short.

Not too drunk.

Not too friendly.

Not too slow.

Not too late.

A severe distrust of men because of my childhood, so says the Freudian-method counsellor after a precise forty-seven minutes of observation and sympathetic nodding. But my childhood was the most innocent time of all. Before the yelling/touching/grabbing/insisting/_____ [insert behaviour of your choice] had even begun.

I went to Italy when I was two and the men smiled at me because I sang *A Pirate's Life for Me* at the top of my lungs as I was pushed down the street.

I went to Italy when I was twenty and the men leered at me because I was blonde and wearing a summer dress that showed off my figure.

And yet –

A father who, while frequently absent in mind and body, never caused me harm. One, two, three older brothers who I see care so deeply for their wives and daughters and sister. Friends; friends who listen to me, who help me, who respect me, and the other women in their lives.

Despite it all, you frighten me. A fear not of the men I know but of the collective *man* that society has me fear just as much as experience does.

Signed,
Me.

FEATHER TOUCH

L. A. TRAYNOR

The men pass by close enough
to brush a hand across a thigh.

Feather touches, a ghost, a
possibility. Dismissed as she

moves through the throng never knowing
the violation her body has endured.

BELOVED MONSTER
OR KEEPING FEAR HEALTHY
BY RHIANNON TATE

EVERYONE HAS A MONSTER...

SOME PEOPLE'S ARE TINY...

SOME PEOPLE'S ARE HUGE...

NEITHER OF THESE ARE HEALTHY. THEY SHOULD BE ABOUT THIS BIG

TO GROW A HEALTHY MONSTER, INTRODUCE IT EARLY AND TRAIN IT WELL

MONSTERS DO BEST ON A DIET OF FAIRY TALES BUT MAKE SURE THEY ARE NUTRITIOUS ONES WHERE THERE ARE BAD GUYS AND SCARY PLACES

HAPPILY—EVERY—AFTERS ARE OK BUT NOT TOO MANY OR THEIR TEETH WILL ROT

IF YOU FEED YOUR MONSTER PROPERLY, IT CAN HELP YOU STRAIGHT AWAY AND WILL KNOW THE DIFFERENCE BETWEEN OLD LADIES AND BAD WITCHES BUT WILL ALWAYS CONSIDER BOTH TO KEEP YOU SAFE

AS YOU GET OLDER, YOUR MONSTER'S DIET WILL CHANGE AND YOU CAN GRADUALLY WEAN IT OFF OF FAIRY TALES AND START GIVING IT BITS OF REAL EXPERIENCE

DON'T WORRY IF YOU THINK THAT MIGHT BE DIFFICULT AS IT IS OK TO KEEP FEEDING IT WITH FAIRY TALES ~ BE SURE TO KEEP THEM WIDELY VARIED FOR OPTIMUM NUTRITION

REMEMBER TO TAKE YOUR MONSTER OUT TO PLAY IF IT STARTS TO GROW TOO BIG...THIS WILL HELP IT GET
SOME EXERCISE AND SHRINK IT DOWN A BIT

IF YOU HAVE GROWN YOUR MONSTER AT A MANAGEABLE RATE FROM EARLY DAYS, IT SHOULD NEVER GET
TOO SMALL BUT IT IS WISE TO CHECK IN OCCASIONALLY ON OTHER PEOPLE'S EXPERIENCES TO SEE
WHAT YOU CAN LEARN FROM THEM AS THIS MIGHT HELP YOUR MONSTER CONTINUE TO KEEP YOU SAFE

~ TROUBLESHOOTING ~

AN OVERGROWN
MONSTER WILL
SMOTHER YOU
AND STOP YOU
HAVING FUN

IT IS HARD WORK
TO SHRINK AN
OVERGROWN MONSTER
BUT WITH PATIENCE,
SUPPORT AND TRAINING
IT CAN BE DONE AND
WILL MAKE YOUR
LIFE EVEN MORE
WONDERFUL

AN UNDERGROWN
MONSTER ISN'T
MUCH USE AND
IS LIKELY TO BE
IGNORED AND ATTACH
ITSELF TO SOMEONE
ELSE

THIS ISN'T FAIR
ON OTHER PEOPLE
WHO END UP ADOPTING
YOUR MONSTER AND
CAN CAUSE YOU TO
BEHAVE IN IMMEASURABLY
SILLY WAYS THAT
CAUSE OTHER PEOPLE'S MONSTERS
TO BECOME OVERGROWN

~ IN SUMMARY ~

YOUR MONSTER SHOULD BE BELOVED BECAUSE ITS
PURPOSE IS TO KEEP YOU SAFE

REMEMBER TO FEED YOUR MONSTER PROPERLY
WHEN YOU ARE SMALL (YOU MAY HAVE TO HELP SMALLER
PEOPLE TAKE CARE OF THEIRS) AND GIVE IT A WIDELY
VARIED DIET OF FAIRY TALES AND EXPERIENCE
AS YOU GROW UP

TRANSLATOR'S PREFACE TO AN UNPUBLISHED WORK

TRANSLATOR'S PREFACE TO AN UNPUBLISHED WORK

CHRIS BEAUSANG

Proposition: History as impersonal as natural disasters, as mute as a quick death, as apologetic as a rising tide.

Proposition: the supersession of the thought of this age by a new Enlightenment of certitude and assurance.

§ 4. History teaches us nothing

 4.1 This is because the vector of history is complacent.

 4.2 Its ignorance w/r/t itself is palpable.

  4.21 Certain manuscripts and artefacts are preserved at the expense of others.

  4.22 Injudicious amounts of radiation leak inconsistently from its constituents.

  4.23 Its preservation of itself is more adequately termed a neglect.

 4.3 We must educate history.

  4.31 We must drill its players in the intricacies of hagiographical doctrine.

  4.32 In this way, history may come to a point of self-knowledge.

   4.321 I dream of cicatrised manuscripts.

   4.322 Carving the irrelevant bits off, quickening their integrates into blushed trauma.

§ 1. It will be noted that this is not an orthodox translator's preface, befitting the text which follows it.

 1.1 It will be noted that this is not an orthodox translation, befitting the preface which precedes it.

 1.2 This preface does not provide an account of the text as such.

§ 2. This text is not a translation; it is a traducement.

    2.1 I do not expect this definitional point to be taken account of by the publisher.

    2.2 I do not expect this definitional point to be taken account of by you.

§ 3. The text is the text.

    3.1 If the text means anything, it means exactly one thing.

§ 5. That we can perceive our image within any historical moment proves there is no end to our vanity.

    5.1 There is a futility to cultural diagnoses.

    5.2 and to *wirkungsgeschichtliches bewußtsein* as such.

§ 6. To speak of declines at any stage of our history is naive.

    6.1 An epoch can only lapse into its proper state.

    6.2 It would be more accurate to speak of restoration.

§ 8. 'Weed' is a relative term, connoting an invasive or unwelcome plant.

    8.1 Something we would rather be without.

    8.2 A weed produces no Rembrandts, delivers no speeches.

    8.3 I would locate in its blankness something to be aspired to.

        8.31 It is not difficult for us to imagine that we may not belong in the pantheon of the civilised.

        8.32 That we may not altogether be, of our own sort.

§ 10. The traducer is as close to native as is possible in this unsanctified age.

§ 11. Accuracy is a tiresome piety.

§ 12. Accuracy is a tiresome luxury.

§ 13. Of each word in this text, a word game was made.

    13.1 Each individual word was written onto a separate piece of paper.

    13.2 These pieces were then arranged into groups of ten.

§ 14. A different Tarot reading was used for each group of ten in order to formulate the mirrored surfaces through which potential meaning was to be refracted.

§ 15. Coins were flipped.

15.1 The coins were used to determine
    15.11 Synonyms
    15.12 Case
    15.13 Gender
    15.14 etc.

§ 16. Translations were carried out based on the alignment of pendula.
    16.1 Augury
        16.11 Hydromancy
        16.12 Tasseography, chiromancy

§ 17. These were used in order to determine the order in which these sections of ten were to be traduced.

§ 18. What you have before you is a far more eclectic text than would have been the case, had I adhered to best practice and the tedium of its attendant metaphysics.

§ 19. I have heard my colleagues speak about words.
    19.1 I have heard them say that they possess their own agency, that they are alive, to a greater extent than we are.
    19.2 We grow old, our bodies prolapse, deaden.
        19.21 I am speaking about myself, but I also speak in an impersonal sense.
        19.22 If I speak of myself, it is accidental.

        —If I am sick it is change that has infected me.
        —My defects are nothing alike.
        —They correspond in the way that one face might present the recollection of another, seeming coeval when participants in the same backdrop of tourmaline grey.
        —They have the fact of me in common and that is all.
        —My brain's tissues are not ulcerative and pockmarked as those of my insides.
        —Tear-shaped picots of serotonin and norepinephrine turning in the synapse's crease, failing and turning, failing and turning, till lost to the janitoring vacuum that fucks everything up, always-already fixing, second by second, the burden of my seeing with these eyes and being in this being.
        —My mind suffers its surfeits; my insides their lack.

19.23 But words, but words.

    19.231 We mustn't blame the body, for sundering to entropy.

        19.2311 They remind us that they are but processes with ends, that these ends are fixed to our own.

19.24 Words, words

    19.241 There is no greater nobility than life spent in the chair, the choosing of these rudiments of indigence, pedantry, and thereby tracing the giddy flashes of the eternal's petticoats.

19.25 Our timescale is not of decades, but thousand-year strata,

    19.251 I am within time-compacted diachronies, my movements as stately and disregarded as those of a continental shelf.

    So spaketh I, owner-proprietor of an inflamed bowel and a broken brain.

19.3 I've heard them spout this dross since the sixties.

19.4 One would have thought that they would be more grateful, having been presented with evidence to this effect.

19.5 I propose on the basis of these words' agency, a rudderless *techne*, a methodology constructed upon falsity.

§ 21. This text has constructed itself.

    21.1 (You will be familiar with this apologia).

§ 22. You may think that you recognise some of what you read here, whether these be complete sentences, or disparate *n*-grams,

    22.1 the particular cant of these sentences.

§ 23. Any parallels are coincidental.

§ 24. Be mindful of literature's mitochondrial eve;

    24.1 language, literature our works, are hopelessly inbred.

———————————

there is a vulgarity to the rolling of a dice mindful of how one's desires hinge upon its outcome.

———————————

One can imagine it, poised within your hand's palm, where its corners may be felt, even as one's grip intensifies around them. Perhaps its solidity is deceptive, and its structure is bringing itself inward, attended by the walls of flesh on each side. It is at this stage easiest to imagine its movement could be the sweep of a lofty and incorporate chance, tiny undulations across a mirror of unprovoked waters. On each return eroded further, refined further, reaching an abjectness in its diminution, nothing of it seeking growth or increase, just an unending maturation without the indignities of decline; a means gracefully thwarted, a reaction quelled. It was the corners that were to betray us all along. When released they clatter as though inept, for you to paw after them, and you think then it would have been better to be where you and the dice were before it was thrown, the number it turned up immaterial, just to feel them there, the corners and their edges, in a uniformity that was finished, and waiting to give way.

I speak in this room without witness, or rather in a room of witnesses indifferent to my voice, which threatens, but never fully extinguishes, the room's vacancy.

The walls are neither yellow nor off-white, but a dereliction of both, even more so at swathes along the floor, broad arcs that broach and thicken at their peaks before dying off, and one wonders what could have happened to have created surfaces that are braised so evenly, as if the room had been flooded, and some sediment had left its residue.

This room has been built for declaiming, but as I stand here, speaking of things that have long ago ceased to matter, in a style that gives the impression that they have not, it seems more fitted to their ends then to mine. Perhaps they too are artefacts of freak weather events, undissipated flecks of condensation. The theatre swells upward and perches them before me, contemptuous as budgerigars, their faces daubed with varying levels of interest, asking questions of me that they lack the wherewithal to pose, which isn't to say that they lack for trying, and as I stand there, trying to unpack what they say, trying to return it to them in a way that might harmonise our understanding, it is not the temperature of the room that rises, but some other, unnamed measure of ambience that ratchets upwards. The room changes, and reveals itself neither fit for me nor them, none of us can be native to a space such as this, wrested beneath the theatre's high ceiling, riveted anomalously with cables in plasticised bundles, reaching across the building, its diversion in and out serving some end, presumably. I speak well, my voice reaches them all, but however capable it is of dealing in prolix abstraction, it is just a question of *when* the sea above us will fall upwards, for us to drown in it.

I have told them Romulus and Remus were not the founders of the city, but its first sackers, purgers of an anaemic and feminised modernity, giving the city over to the steady desecration of nature. Some horde of barbarians rampaging through the forum was not as permanent a solution as they required, for they foresaw an age in which the ruins would be preserved, the stones sold, and wished instead for the temples, expressive of a tyranny of order to be vanquished by the anarchic tendencies of a spreading vine, because the vine has no centre; the barbarian mind could be trusted, but it could not be *believed*. Rome did not fall when it was sacked, it rather rose, not a suicide but its ethical opposite, keeling over and allowing oneself to seep out of existence. They saw also, for they were not idiots, in their own will, a tyranny that could not be ceded to, and they realised between themselves a death pact, their followers left to carry out their vision. Rome entered a second pre- history as a sequence of disaggregated municipalities on hillsides, edging nearer the brothers' vision of a desynoecised Rome, its residua to be consumed by flora and fauna. Far from laying the germ of our greatest civilisation, they were its first destroyers, visionary apocalyptists, the inventors of the end of the world. And it was the real deal back then, not the facile veneer that it has taken on now, this was no anthropocene, hundreds of years of contradiction reaching its necessary terminus, this was the end of the world as *task*, as a civic *project*. I have told them all this. I have told them their greatest emperor was an Ægyptian freeman, I have told them Roman history warns us of the dangers of parliamentary democracy, I have told them a prosperous nation and a strong people requires the blood of its citizens. I have told them Rome did not exist, that the city was an invention of bourgeois intellectuals in the fifties, that Rome was an act of will, I have told them everything, and everything was a lie. Which they accept, because the tally of what they know about anything reaches something around the figure of perfect zero.

I live unhistorically, not because I wish to.

F.

FRANTICALLY FLEEING THE FEDS
FLYING FROM FREEWAY TO FREEWAY
FEROCIOUSLY FIGHTING FOR FREEDOM

FLIPSIDE

FEELINGS FERMENTED IN FORGOTTEN FIGHTS
FRANTICALLY FAKING A FINE F.T
FORMULAIC, FORCED TO FIND THE FRONT

FOG

FEMINISTS FACE FACISTS, FORGE FRIENDSHIPS,
FIND FAMILY
FELLAS FLOAT FAR FROM THE FOLD
FOREVER FEART TO FOLLOW.

PAMERON FOSTER
FEBRUARY ISH 2017

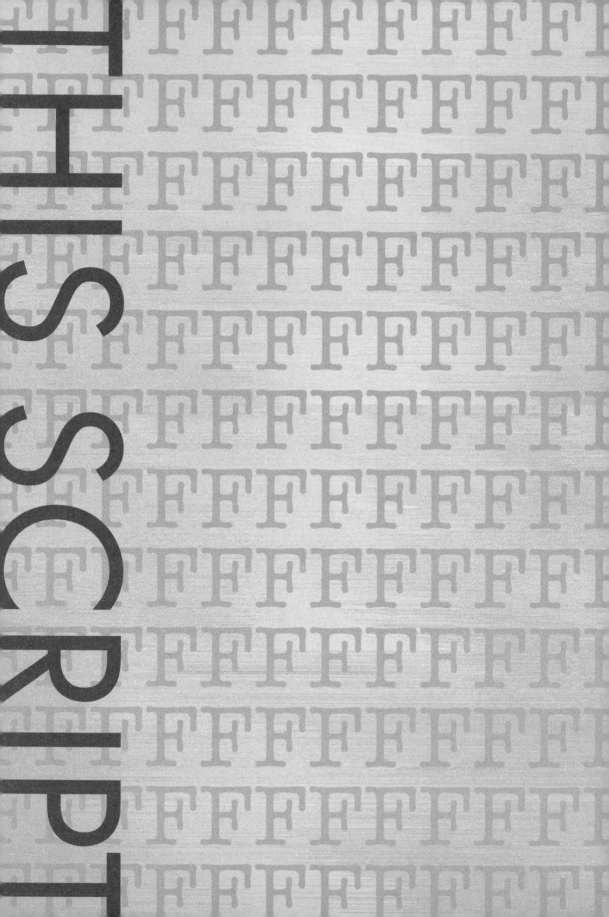

THIS SCRIPT

THIS SCRIPT
(A PART-UNIVOCALISM IN, AND ABOUT I)

JENNY LINDSAY

Since six, it imprints in skin.
This 'girl' script.
This birth-right, which kills spirit.

Whilst timid lips twitch, '*Shh, girls;*
swirl mildly within this!'
'I's itch in this skin; in this script.

Misfits spit:
"*Kill this!*
Whip nit-wits stingingly with livid riffs!
This script stinks!
It is shirt lifts, it is skirt shims with impish grins!
It is slits pink, bikini tits,
It is pricks infringing with victim scripts!
It is in birth 'til infirm; this script, this 'girlish' mimicry.

Grim risk, if girls wish trim bits within knicks;
If thigh-ripping "thick-skins" in big biff shirts; if bits binding
in rigid, distinct, ticks-in-identifying-with-scriptish-wish-lists is INSPIRING??

Pft!

It binds 'I' within slim-picking, piddling limits!"

Misfits flick digits, fists twitch, indignity fizzes, sighs rising.

'I, girl' – is it implicit? Is it I.D?
This insipid script, is it simply *right*? Writ in birth, identity: *'cis'*?

Irrrrr......Is this misprint?

Pft.
Quit it.
Stick it in bins brimming with skin flicks.
High-five other 'I's, let a collective "I" light up within winning shin-kickings!

Bitches, reclaim this script – be singing:
"One is not born, one becomes a woma….."

Oops!
Off script…

Illicit thinking – skirting kinship with siblings, whilst
hissing indignity within 'isms' splits I.D from 'I's;
Schisms rip Twit'ring vigils – timid girls flit, sighing
"Skirmish? Irk. Pitching in is visibility, crisis rid! Shhhhhh….."

Kick it.
This script is I-ridden. 'I' is limiting. 'I' is I, first; tight-knit wiring gives wind-chill.

We are not this script.
Though we act it well, and with vim…

'I' stands still, individual, while a collective head wricks nccks to listen.

THE FIRST TIME

THE FIRST TIME

RICKY MONAHAN BROWN

Wow. It's really quiet. Why's it so quiet?

And everyone's looking at me.

Why is everybody looking at me?

Mr O'Dell is looking right at me. The big vein on his forehead has popped, and his big bug eyes are popping out of his big, bald head. And his big, bald head is popping out of his stupid black turtleneck. What a cock.

Still. This can't be good.

'Ms Morgenstern...?'

I knew it.

'Would you like to pick up for us?'

'Uh... yeah... sure...'

I talk in slow motion while I swipe up at speed, looking for a word, a phrase, anything that might trigger something. It's kind of hard with Tiffany craning around in her chair in front of me, mindlessly chewing gum and enjoying the show. I'm mortified. Kieron must think I'm a total idiot.

No, he wouldn't think that.

Man, I've just been sitting here, daydreaming. Contemplating the butterflies in my stomach about what we're going to do. If I clench my thigh muscles, I can make the butterflies go mad, and my heart sploshes around in my guts. It sounds gross, but I like it.

There. Just like that.

The butterflies tell me that if I kick away one of the back legs of the bucket chair Tiffany's swinging on, she'll fall backwards and her head will smash into my desk with a sickening thud.

It turns out the butterflies are right.

How can she be captain of the cheerleading team with such shitty balance? The butterflies do a little dance of celebration. O'Dell is less happy.

'Ms Naylor. What the hell is going on with you?'

'But... but... Darla...'

She can hardly form the words in a fog of nausea and rage.

'I don't know what you're trying to say, Ms. Naylor, but I do know that Ms Morgenstern, for all her numerous faults, isn't swinging on her chair and breaking school property.'

O'Dell deciding that he's on my team in this one buys me a pardon. Urgh.

'Act 4, scene 5, Darla?' he winks. 'Line 34...? *Ready to go...?*'

'Uh, yeah.'

There it is –

'Ready to go, but never to return
O son! The night before thy wedding day
Hath death lain with thy wife. The she lies,
Flower as she was, deflowered by him.'

'Thank you, Ms Morgenstern.'

Screw you, creep.

'Now, for tomorrow – the questions are in your iPads. How does Paris feel about Juliet's death? How does Friar Lawrence comfort Juliet's family? What does *Ready to go but never to return* mean after Paris...'

BRRRRRRRRINNG!!!!!!!

Thank god. You can picture the scene, right? The school bell tears through the halls of Pleasant Valley High. There's a second of silence, then a roiling teenage mass explodes out of the classrooms, shouting and roughhousing and slamming locker doors. Kieron and I are the first ones out of O'Dell's English Lit classroom. We've been surreptitiously packing our bags at the back of the class so when the bell rings, we're able to stride between the desks, ignoring Tiffany and Joely and Jack-o and Chuckles and all the other interchangeable bags of hormones stuffing away all their shit.

We stop at Kieron's locker, so he can dump off the accumulated crap of another wasted day and pick up his bag. I throw in my shit as well. We're, like, sharing a locker now? It saves us having to schlep all the way across school when we're just trying to get the hell outta here. It's our common locker, but he still keeps that picture of me stuck inside the door. I don't like the way I look in the picture, but Kieron always says he likes it.

'Are you sure you're OK with this, Darla?' he asks me.

'Oh, yeah. Definitely. I'm just a bit... nervous.'

'Huh. Yeah. I know what you mean. I meant it, you know. I've never done anything like this before, either.'

The butterflies start dancing in my stomach again. They feel good, almost like little explosions of joy. But I still kinda want to barf. Kieron looks nervous, too. I think. I mean, I dunno. How can you ever know what someone else is thinking?

I guess you've got to use your words.

Oh god, Darla. *You're so deep.*

Kieron uses his words. Oh, Kerry. That's why I like, *like you* like you, Baby.

'So. Where do you want to do it first?' he asks. 'We could go to your dad's house, raid his stash of joints, get a little relaxed before we get down to business?'

'No way! I mean, can you imagine him blundering in like Cliff Huxtable or something? Trying to make it into *A Very Special Episode of Blossom?*'

'What the hell is *A Very Special Episode of Blossom?*'

'Oh, *Blossom* was this ancient sitcom that would occasionally have these "Very Special Episodes" to raise parents' kids for them.'

'What?! I coulda used that!'

'No shit, Kerry. Make out parties are *not* mandatory. And get this, there was one where Blossom, like, sees a gun in her classmate's locker and calls a tip line to report him. Then the school searches his locker, but finds nothing. He threatens Blossom for ratting on him. And at the end of the episode, you find out that Jimmy died after an "accident with his gun."'

'Omigod! That's hilarious! Hey. Heads up. Incoming at seven o'clock.'

Kieron nods over my shoulder. It's just Laine. Laine's OK.

'Hey, Darla, Ker. Whatcha doin? Wanna give me a ride to Chico's? I hear the new season's accessories are off the chain.'

It's an in-joke. You wouldn't get it. Anyway, as well as being the school quarterback − dating me, I know! − Kieron's got this sweet car. People are always angling for a ride. I mean, Laine's OK, but some of those freeloaders...

'I'd love to, Laine'   I would *not* love to, not right now − 'but Ker and I need to talk.'

I flash her a meaningful look − 'I'll meet you there? Go on now, git.'

Laine gits. Phew!

'No, let's do it in O'Dell's classroom first. Creepy bastard.'

'Are you kidding me, Darla?!'

I am *not* kidding. We stride back into O'Dell's room. He's still there, organizing papers and tidying his desk.

'Ms Morgenstern, Mr Sampson. Leave something behind?'

'No, O'Dell, you creepy fuck. I just don't like the way you perv over my woman, yeah?'

We stay standing at the door, and Kieron takes our matching AR-15s − *America's gun* − out of his bag and passes me one.

Mr O'Dell's the first.

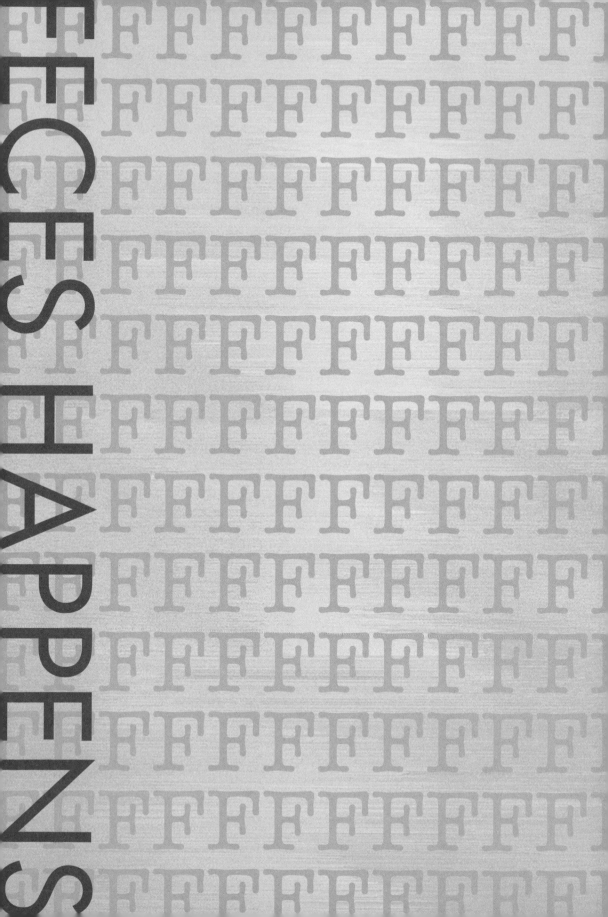

FECES HAPPENS

FECES HAPPENS

REX BROMFIELD

Day 1

When I got home Monday evening I was really beat. A big design project was up and the architectural firm I work for had everyone scrambling to get the bid in. I was so exhausted that I fell onto the sofa without getting my usual Bud from the fridge.

I didn't really notice it at first – the smell, that is – it was faint. I thought I'd left the balcony door ajar and it was drifting in from outside. But strange smells like that don't usually make it up to the fourteenth floor. I hauled myself out of my collapse to get the beer and close the door.

Wait a minute.

Right there, half way to the kitchen, at the bathroom, the smell got stronger. I sniffed by the door, leaned in, turned on the light and sniffed again.

Whew!

Damn, had I actually gone out that morning and forgotten to flush? That's not like me. But there it was, sitting heavily in the bottom of my high-tech minimum-flow toilet bowl. It was a turd the size of a short two-by-four curled up like it was asleep.

I flushed it then washed my hands.

Twice.

How could this be? I quickly reviewed my morning routine. Get out of bed; pajamas off; shorts; T-shirt; put on coffee; brush teeth; wash face; drink coffee; move bowels; flush; shave; shower; comb hair; dress; wallet; cellphone; briefcase; socks; shoes; out the door. Flushing was definitely part of the routine.

I got the Bud, put on the TV and forgot about it.

I woke up twice during the night, the first time to pee, the second time from a crazy dream where Janice Miles, whom I share an office with, and the only female technologist in the company, was selling bathroom fixtures to restaurateurs. This was crazy because Janice is quite respected in the firm and wouldn't be doing something as mundane as pitching bathroom fixtures.

Day 2

On Tuesday morning a rumor went around that another firm might get the job, after all, so everybody kind of relaxed a bit. All I had to do was make a few adjustments to an outside plaza that Ken Wells, one of the pickier partners, had come up with at lunch. The changes to the drawings took about twenty minutes. As an architectural technologist, I actually get to do some of the creative work. The partners will often claim your work as theirs when it's good and blame you when something screws up. Welcome to the biz. That's why I'm careful. So I can move up in the firm one step at a time.

Like I said, the day was easy and I felt like working a bit on my personal project when I got home Tuesday night. Every junior architect has their own spare-time pet project that they hope will eventually see the light of day.

I opened a Bud and was booting up my laptop when there it was again, that faint and wispy suggestion that I may be downwind of a sewage treatment plant. I went straight into the bathroom to see what was going on – not that anything was going on, *it* was just sitting there. Damn, I'd forgotten to flush *again*. I hit the handle and down the offender went. This time, I sprinkled some cleanser into the bowl and brushed it clean, then flushed again and opened the balcony door to blow the stink out of the place.

I tried to do some work but my mind kept returning to the details of my morning routine.

I tossed and turned all night.

Day 3

On Wednesday we got word that the firm had been awarded the contract. Nobody was going to have to worry about their jobs now. In fact, there might even be promotions. The project was a thirty-seven story, mixed-use, structure for the downtown core. Two cases of champagne were delivered in the morning and everybody stuck around after five for the party.

The whole time I was talking to Janice Miles, I was looking over her shoulder and out the window to where I could just see the top corner of my building ten blocks away. I wasn't paying attention to what she was saying. I had flushed that morning, hadn't I? Yes, I was sure because I deliberately broke my routine by going back and flushing a second time. At one point I think Janice became a bit irritated with me and mentioned something about me being anal and walked away. I heard that part because of the word *anal*. It's not at all like me to ignore Janice, but I simply couldn't concentrate. I considered going after her to apologize, but I wanted to get home and make sure things had returned to normal.

I always take off my shoes when I come into the apartment. Not this time. This time, I went straight into the bathroom. Sure enough, just like yesterday and the day before, there it was, curled up like some fat, sleeping anaconda, smugly secure in its casual defilement of my private retreat. My blood pressure rose. I leaned on the flush handle so hard that, for a moment, I thought I'd broken it. Down the offending excrement went. What the hell *was* this? I poured half a bottle of bleach into the toilet bowl and flushed again, repulsed by the acrid encore.

Okay, I had to get a handle on this, but standing staring into the toilet wasn't going to do it. I put the lid down, washed my hands, then went to the kitchen to get a Bud.

Damn. I was all out. Do I dare leave the apartment for a few minutes to get a six-pack?

I waited for the elevator to come, but when it did I felt compelled to let it go and return to make sure I'd locked the door to my apartment.

At the corner convenience store, a thought suddenly struck. I picked up a six-pack, raced back home, peeled the superintendent's magnetized card from the fridge door and dialed his number. I asked if he'd done any work in my suite that day. He actually had to look it up. His job must be more demanding than I thought. No, he hadn't been in my place in over three months. He was careful to remind me that he never entered a tenant's unit without permission.

I got the flashlight from the kitchen tool drawer and went out into the hall to check the lock on the front door. Not even so much as a scratch where someone might have jimmied their way in.

I had to think. Lay things out in a logical fashion and figure out the motives and methodology of this revolting incursion. Relieving oneself, uninvited, at the personal comfort station of another surely is a home invasion of sorts, isn't it? I was being held hostage under my own roof by a deliberate act of biological vandalism. What could anyone hope to gain by surreptitiously defecating in the restroom of another, then sneaking away down some back stairs and...?

The back stairs!

I went down the hall to the fire exit, had a good look one floor up and two down. No clue.

I double locked my door and sank onto the sofa. I don't know why, but I felt that nothing had been touched – certainly not the toilet flush lever. Did I know how to engage a forensic investigator who could lift prints from the front door handle? Then what? On TV they lift prints with something that looks like big scotch tape then put it into a three-hundred thousand dollar machine then...

I was being ridiculous.

I put on the TV, tried to clear my mind, but my thoughts swirled around like the time I drank three Buds *and* took the sleeping pill by mistake. Eventually, I fell asleep askew in front of some generic police show.

I dreamt that I was mugged in the street by two thugs who escorted me down to the lakefront where they flushed me away off the end of a small pier.

I awoke with my head at ninety degrees to the rest of my body. My neck felt like it was full of twisted re-bar. The apartment looked strange. Had I over-extended myself buying this place? I really didn't need *two* bedrooms *or* the sunken living room. Couldn't really do much in that fancy kitchen either. Maybe someday I'd get lucky and meet the right girl and all this will mean something. The layout was suitably impressive. Anyone could see that I was capable of taking care of myself and, therefore, a family. Now, it felt empty and cold in some way, strange and foreign, violated.

Day 4

On the walk to work, I began to wonder if I should call the police. And tell them what exactly? That someone broke into my house and took a dump in my toilet? I'm sure they would be eager to have their top detectives thoroughly investigate *that* allegation. My call would more likely be recorded and leaked onto the internet in no time. I would be an international laughing stock. I may have been thinking out loud. I was getting strange looks.

I was distracted at work. I stared at my computer screen until Ken Wells leaned in and told me to open the plaza in the new design a bit more. Something about making the entrance more inviting. I got the project file on the screen and unconsciously moved the base of a dozen columns apart by a couple of metres, then, without thinking about what I was doing, moved them again. When I noticed the impossible load distribution, not to mention the ridiculous visual effect sloping pillars had on what had been a nice plain exterior walkway, I slid them back. But I had only done half of them when it occurred to me that anyone surreptitiously pooping in my potty would need a key, not only to my apartment but to the building. Eric, the doorman. He would have seen something.

I threw my revisions onto the hard drive of the company's main server and left work early. Showing up unexpectedly at 3:30 instead of at 5:30 might just surprise the culprit himself.

Eric, the doorman, laughed when I asked if he'd seen anyone strange or suspicious. He told me he saw strange people and suspicious at his job all the time. He reminded me that this is midtown. But as soon as he saw that I was serious, his smile dissolved away and he assured me that no one who does not belong in the building ever gets past him.

I lingered in the shadows watching Eric until I realised that now I really *was* being crazy. Why the hell would the doorman sneak into *my* apartment on the fourteenth floor to relieve himself when there was a perfectly good washroom in the service room down here? Anyway, Eric would have flushed.

Entering my site, I almost didn't notice the malodorous tendril, reaching out, welcoming me home. But there it was again, as usual. It looked a little bigger than before and when I flushed, for a moment I thought it wasn't going to go down. I know these toilets are designed not to overflow but the anxiety welled up anyway, and when the plug suddenly let go, a speck of the liquid waste sprang up hitting me right in the middle of my left cheek.

I took a long, scalding shower, drank two quick, medicinal beers, then went to stretch out on my bed to think things through once and for all.

Day 5

I was so exhausted and upset that I slept the rest of the afternoon and right through the night. Now, sunlight streaming in, I was already late for work. No time to shave or shower. I pulled myself together as best I could and ran out. Without my morning coffee, I was unable to move my bowels until I got to the office. Now I wasn't even using my own toilet.

I looked at myself in the men's room mirror. I could have been one of those guys who asks you for money in the street.

I returned to my office, trying to stay out of general view. Luckily Janice didn't even look up. But right away here came Ken Wells waving a large colour printout. At first, I thought he was angry, but instead, he was all excited. He thought the pillars were fantastic and asked how on Earth I'd ever come up with the idea. I had to admit that the columns staggered all over like that did look pretty... energetic. What he really wanted to know was how I'd still managed to carry the loads correctly with this new airy rearrangement. But all the while I was watching Janice as she inspected my design. It was weird. After that, she looked at me and talked to me in a completely different way than she ever had before. She even asked me what I thought of her sketch for a swimming pool design. That was something she'd *never* done. For some reason, I suggested she fill all the non-support structure with glass so it felt more out in the open. She stared at me for a long time, then went back to her desk and started working feverishly.

On my way out that night, Don Milton and Ken Wells stopped me at the elevator and asked me to join them for a cocktail.

By the time I got home I was pretty high with creative energy, the suggestion of a promotion and three or four Manhattans. I don't remember getting undressed and going to bed but I guess I did because I awoke on Saturday morning around nine, in my pajamas, in bed.

I put on the coffee and was in the middle of brushing my teeth when it all came flooding back to me. I opened the toilet lid and looked in.

Nothing.

And now I remembered. There had been *nothing* in the toilet the night before when I got home. I knew this because I threw up after wolfing down a peanut butter and marmalade sandwich on a burnt onion bun as soon as I got in. You'd remember something like a monster turd staring you in the face when you're down on your knees at the bowl like that.

I made some coffee. Stood at the window. Looked out at the city and thought something I'd never thought before. *That skyline could definitely use some improvement.* I smiled myself a self-satisfied smile and sipped my coffee.

I was feeling pretty good.

At exactly 10:00 AM the phone rang.

I didn't know Janice had my phone number.

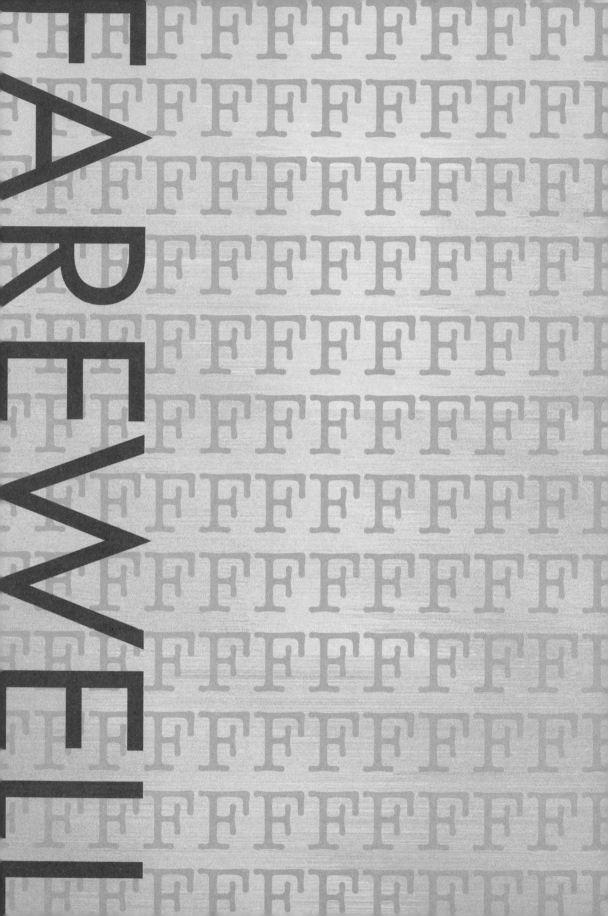

FAREWELL

FAREWELL

CALUM MACLEOD

Air an Ochdamh latha phriont i
a-mach an cead-bòrdaidh RyanAir
agus thug i a cead-siubhail bhon drathair
ann an dorchadas na moch-thrath

Air an Ochdamh latha fhuair i
bus chun Aerfoirt
oir cha robh guth aice
ri ràdh ri fear tagsaidh

Air an Ochdamh latha ghabh i
deoch is poca Tayto Cheese
and Onion, is choimhead i
na bùird agus na litrichean dhearg

Air an Ochdamh latha shuidh i
na cathair, anns an fhicheadamh
riadh, ri taobh pàiste
nach sgurradh a caoineadh

Air an Ochdamh latha ràinig i
Liverpool.

Agus air an an Ochdamh latha dh'fhàg i
Liverpool.

Air an Ochdamh latha thìll i
a cead-siubhal dhan drathair
ann an dorchadas na h-oidhche

So fair thee well, my own true love
When I return united we will be
It's not the leaving of Liverpool that grieves me
But my darling, when I think of thee.

GOOD APPLES

GOOD APPLES

EVA CARSON

Terrible weather. Fucking freezing. Horrible. He was going to the Asda on the way home and he was going to get everything he needed, and he was not going to bother his arse going back out. That would be him for the weekend. Hibernation, basically.

Soon as he walked in the door the guy was watching him. Wee smile on him as if: I know your type. I'm onto you, son. But for a start he was in his fucking work clothes. The name of the company, sewn over the left breast of his fleece. He was hardly about to

It was ever since what happened to his face. He knew that. Nothing personal.

Except it was him that had to deal with it day in day out just folk looking at you like you're a

Anyway.

He should have written a shopping list so he had something to focus on. Because he should have known. He should have known this was going to be difficult. Jesus folk just staring at you and

Start where you are. Where was he? In the fruit aisle. Okay. Just picking up a bag of apples and just putting them in his basket and looking over and the guard still watching him. I am not stealing the apples you fucking

Right, so this was him in the place two minutes and his head was bouncing. He needed to calm down. But the place wasn't helping. It was lit up like a fucking interrogation room. And weans screaming and running about and it was nearly Christmas so they all had that greedy light in their eyes and there was music stuck on a screaming loop in the ceiling and the screaming weans and the folk rattling the trolleys about and the guy watching him.

Woman next to him, with her hand in about the tangerines, pausing and looking up at him. Sliding her eyes across his face. Taking her time over it. Zoo exhibit.

Someone else looking at him now. Wee old man.

I'm not some kind of monster I didn't plan on this it's just what happened to me and

Security guard peering over. Frowning a bit because he was losing him in the crowd of the fruit aisle.

Jesus sweet living Christ he was not stealing apples!

Calm down. He wasn't like this. This wasn't him.

He remembered what it had been like when he'd been invisible. Fierce stab of nostalgia for when he'd been invisible.

The apples with union jacks printed on the plastic bag. Good British Apples, the label said.

Fucksake.

Into the aisle with the soup and the beans and at least the clown on the door hadn't followed him. Soup was good, you could live off that no hassle. Weans running past him and past the soup.

Round the corner to the biscuits. Custard creams. Three packets because they're on a deal.

Detour back round towards the electricals bit where no doubt he would be accused of trying to shove an iPad up his shirt but still no sign of the door guy and he had a wee look at the DVDs. You could see anything you wanted online but they still sold these DVDs and you stood looking at them thinking it was a treat, you might treat yourself to a wee DVD.

Whole big massive display of TVs on a huge wall, right up twenty feet in the air, and all the screens showing the same thing. Some sort of nature documentary and it was horrible, it was this lizard swallowing another lizard, taking its time over it with cold bulging eyes and its mouth all stretched out. That's what they were showing you on fifty different screens. Really festive.

Security guard cruising past with his eyes narrowed.

That's a good one, a woman's voice said.

Turning his head towards her, and her jumping and actually gasping. Her hand fluttering at her chest like something out of an old horror film.

Her saying she was sorry.

Him saying it was okay.

He looked down at the DVD in his hands. She was already stepping back. She smiled and fucked off into the video game bit. He put the DVD back on the display.

Christ. Just waves of a really bleak feeling.

Picking up a couple of bottles of vodka, and a bottle of cola. Crisps and nuts. Bread. Cheese. And that was him. He could leave any time he wanted. He had what he needed.

He shouldn't be getting the drink but it didn't matter.

Just keep the head down and get to the till and that was it done. He should be making a list of these things, the counsellor said. Writing down the things he'd managed to do.

Managed to go for a shop without losing the fucking heid. Tick. Smiley face. That's what she'd actually said: put a wee smiley face next to it.

Managed to go for a shop without being reminded that he was an unfuckable monstrosity. Naw. Big red cross. Sad face. Sad, ugly fucking face.

He was nearly at the top of the queue when he realised he didn't have a paper. Just, he would get that half-cut desire for a wee bit of self improvement and want to read the news and he'd be annoyed if he didn't have a paper. Online wasn't the same, you picked out the stuff you wanted then you skimmed the rest and then you were into the porn.

He cut back out the queue and there was the security guard swimming about in the crowd. Smirk on his face like: I knew you joining the queue was a bluff, son.

Christ!

Take the apples out of the basket, the good British apples. Start pelting him with them. Cause a scene. Give everyone something to look at.

The newspaper stand was at the door. The guard taking up his wee spot by the promotional mince pies. Just watching.

Head down and looking at the papers. Terrible selection in the place. It was all terror of immigrants. Filthy cheating poor. House prices. The fucking Royal Family. More immigrants. A celebrity he didn't recognise. In a bikini, in December, on the front page. Bikini red and white like Santa. Good hips. Good legs.

Where were the big papers?

There were no blank spaces on the stand. It wasn't like they'd sold out. Where were they putting the big papers? Maybe there was another display.

Couldn't see one. Christ. This big box of a place, teeming round him. It must make fucking thousands. It sold twenty different types of jam and there were no big papers. All this stuff, all being munched by readers of this shite. And all these toys for their weans, as well! Just aisles and aisles of it. They were reproducing!

He should alert his old pal the security guard. Get him to call the management down.

Good sir, I should like to register a complaint. All your biscuits are being eaten by fascists!

Rivers of jam and blood!

The guard still staring at him and folk just staring and

Just fucking everyone teeming round him and the weans and the noise and the light.

FEROCIOUS

LANGUAGE

FEROCIOUS LANGUAGE

SIOBHAN DUNLOP

Don't swear, they tell you,
aged too young to know the best words,
and it sticks, like a plaster on a scuffed knee.

Bloody, bum, boobies:
five year olds giggle, innocent of why
their sound has a nervous edge, tainted.

One shit and it's everywhere.
Oh shit. The children heard, the ones
with a greater interest in shit than most.

A wanker, a twat, what a dick
that guy is, mouthing off down his phone
on the bus into town, where anyone can hear him.

Secondary school walls
coated in cocks like pens have a mind
of their own. Words etched into old desks. Fuck.

Fuck indeed. Fucking
hell, fuck's sake, fuck off, fuck you:
the act of using 'fuck' as versatile as the act.

The big one, the reclaimed,
the intolerably offensive, the 'in Britain
we use it differently'. He's a good cunt really.

Words have power.
Some attack, offend, belittle, exclude,
and some are just fucking everywhere.

BED REST BY

ELEANOR ULDRIDGE

BED REST BY ELEANOR ULDRIDGE

ERROL RIVERA

--a few weeks ago, my son came home for the very first time. His name is Gibson, and he is by far the best smelling thing to ever come out of me. I'd even say that he looks like me, but I'm still recovering from labour and frankly I'm not that cruel. So, until I can wash my hair and sleep through a whole night, he'll have to settle for looking like his father.

"Work junkie" is the term most often stapled to me. Mostly by my husband, Bryan, who is as patient as he is fertile, and by my editor, Julie. Her card mentioned how grateful she was that I didn't try to send her any articles in between contractions.

I couldn't write now if I wanted. Not since Brian and I brought Gibson home from the hospital. Some new mothers need to stay in bed for weeks, I'm told. That's plenty of time for me to deliver a few overdue articles.

But I've got nothing.

I can write in the make-up room of the mayor's favourite strip club while girls named after cocktails do lines off Waitrose catalogues. I can write while 1,800 student activists get drunk and dance like morons for a free Tibet.

I can write with a baby.

It's the bed. This bed they say I have to stay in. I didn't bat an eye when they told me I'd poop in a room full of strangers while giving birth, but bed rest?

Are you insane?

It's not the stories I'm missing that's the problem – it's the stories that find me. Because I have to stay sharp. I have to keep working, but there's only one story I can think of.

My stories are the only ones I swear I'd never write, but I think I there's a way around that. Because it's not I just my story, or Owen's. It's also her's.

It's never bothered me that I look like my mother, but now I'm afraid I'm beginning to see like her too.

Because this is a story we share now, right?

Now, more than ever, I guess.

Because, like me, she was also uneasy with bed rest.

Like me – at least for a time.

So here it goes.

* * *

Bed Rest
By Eleanor Uldridge

In the spring of 1986 our bedroom window faced the sunrise. I'd roll over and wake John by pulling back the big brown curls of his hair. I liked to lay on his chest and see my little plastic statue of the Virgin Mary.

John brought it back from his mother's in Spain. He said it was a gift from her. It came with a little plastic crown to fit on top of her head. There was something about the way that little statue of Mary looked at the baby in her hands. It wasn't a happy look.

And it wasn't a sad one either.

Just soft.

Most days, I'd say morning prayers, kiss John, get up, and place the little crown on Mary's head. At night, just before bed, I'd take the crown off, place it on the dresser, and have prayer.

I did this every day until eventually, I think I was afraid of what would happen if I didn't. When the crown disappeared, I probably panicked. I can't be sure if that's when it started. All I know is that one day, John brought me tea in bed.

Eleanor, Ellie, was eight and she had started to get ready for school by herself, but Owen, little Owen, he still needed help. One day the kids climbed onto the bed, all dressed for school, and hugged me goodbye.

Did John dress them?

When?

Why didn't he ask me to help?

Did he ask me?

'Are you sick, sweety?' he must have said.

'Must be,' I think I said.

I started to sleep for weeks.

I was just so tired.

There are those moments after you wake up, when you realize there's more than you, that you're in a bed, and that the bed ends, and there's a whole day beyond the edge of it. You'd make any deal, trade any precious thing to stay where you are. I clung to those moments like someone strapped me to them.

They lasted for hours.

They lasted for days.

More and more often, I'd wake up without John next to me. Just see my little plastic Mary on the dresser. What was that look? Is that how a mother is supposed to look at her child? Like they're God? Did I look at my child like that? Did I have to?

I'd see the little baby in her arms, and I'd call out for Ellie. She would tell me all about her baby brother's drawings, or lull me to sleep with one of her little stories.

The poor thing.

She loves to tell stories.

Sometimes, I'd wake to find Dr. Marsh looming over me with his stethoscope. When he finished with me, he'd smile. Then I'd hear him and John whispering in the hall. They strategized, like two interrogators trying to break a liar.

I wondered how long before Ellie would be on their side.

Some days I'd wake up and never open my eyes.

'Are you awake, Mommy?' Owen had learned to ask.

He'd run and jump into my warm bed.

Then something inside me would remember what it was like to be awake with my son. I'd hold Owen, with my eyes closed, and when I opened them I'd see her – that Eleanor.

She was standing in the hallway. She'd stand there staring, like I wasn't what mothers were. But I looked at my children just like my Mary and her little soft plastic face. I was looking at my children like I was plastic and the children were plastic too.

Then something inside me would roll over and go back to sleep. I was just so tired. John worked later hours and I'm sure he was glad to at first. Until the day after sunset, when I woke to clinking and clattering in the kitchen.

I didn't think much of it. Sometimes the neighbours came over to make dinner for the kids. With a pillow against one ear, and the void of sleep still pulling back on me, surely I could hear the children's voices through the bedroom door. My eyes probably didn't widen at the sound of crashing pots and breaking dishes. Breaking glass?

Little Owen cried out. I could hear everything finally. I could hear my son's sobbing and my daughter's scream as it filled the house. I could even hear her struggle to drag his soft little body over broken bits on the floor. Definitely glass.

Eleanor ran up the stairs, calling out to me. In the moonlight I could see Mary. She looked so sleepy.

Down the hall Eleanor came on her fast little feet – followed briefly by a moment of silence – then a thud. A crack maybe? A crack against the wall? Yes – just outside our bedroom.

It shook the dresser, and Mary slid onto the floor.

Ellie couldn't make words any more. She wailed. Coughing and choking on her own tears I'd think. I listened to her bang on the wall with her tiny palms as I rolled over and went back to sleep.

* * *

Brian knows all this, of course. He asked about the scar on my forehead and it all just came out. That was on our second date. Christ, It's a miracle I'm married at all. But now I'm not sure if he remembers. Why would he? It's been so long, and he's paying so much attention to the baby. He probably can't see the look on my face.

I hope he sees it soon. Because Bryan goes back to work tomorrow, and Gibson is waking up. I can hear him stirring. Any second he'll start crying. And the only thing I can think, is that I'm just so tired.

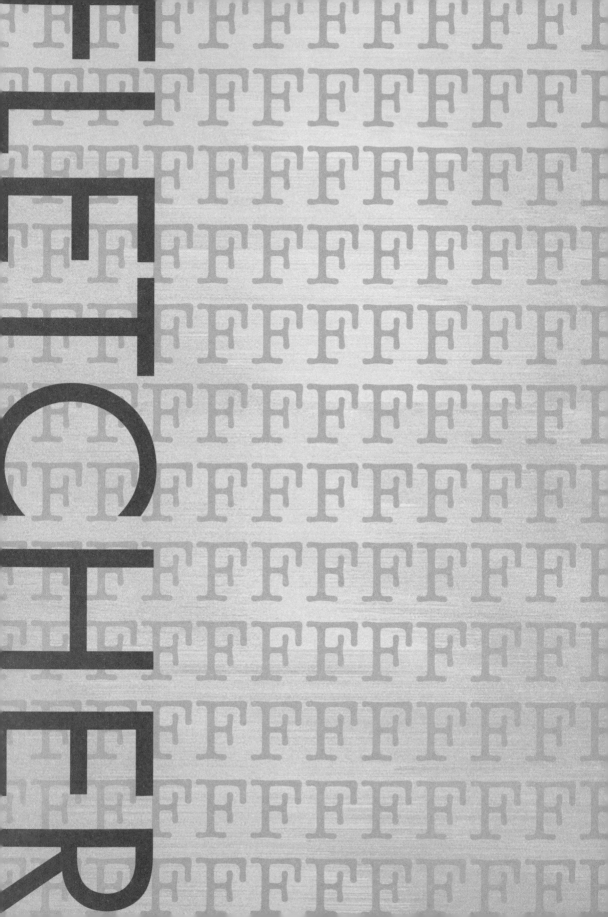

FLETCHER

VERONIQUE KOOTSTRA

Paula Webster, known to her clients as Jessica, walks around the body of 'The Mayor' lying on the garage floor. She assesses the Jackson Pollock-esque scene. She'd unintentionally added a splash of colour to the lawnmower. The blood had squirted out like a defunct sprinkler as she slit his throat. This is what her clients want; a realistic, gory murder scene. On her website she describes her murder mystery game as: 'a unique experience you'll never forget.' She wrote this when she was still using fake blood and a blow-up doll, but she got bored of pretending. She needed some excitement; her job at a call centre was slowly destroying her soul.

The theme music from Murder, She Wrote blares from the stereo. Paula had stood behind the workbench (wearing her Jessica Fletcher wig and latex gloves) theatrically pushing the keys on her typewriter when Jimbo swaggered in, holding up two bottles of beer and his character card. All that was left of Jimbo's mayor chain were skeletons of chocolate coin wrappers. *Greedy bastard.* Paula had made the right choice. Besides, Jimbo was the only one on the guestlist without a proper name. Paula knew people with nicknames and they were all arseholes.

'Thanks for killing me. I cannae be arsed. Nae offense.'

'None taken. Just lie down,' Paula pointed at the empty space next to the lawnmower. She traced the outline of his body with a piece of chalk.

'So, whodunit then?' Jimbo finished both beers simultaneously before lying down.

'That would ruin the game. Just relax.' She covered his eyes with a sleeping mask. Paula unfolded the towel concealing a breadknife. The latex gloves served as a second skin, masking her sweaty fingers.

Paula straightens her wig, presses 'play' on the stereo and jabs at the typewriter keys.

pop   science

politics   the arts

FEMME MAGNIFIQUE
TAKING NAMES AND CHANGING THE GAME

If you're frustrated by what's happening in the world right now, from the sudden jeopardy of women's rights to the overall global negativity, join us in creating FEMME MAGNIFIQUE, a book that dares to turn the tables.

This is the battle cry that sat atop the project's Kickstarter page in early 2017, and rallied over 1,700 people to their cause. They needed $40,000 to make the book a reality. They ended up just shy of $100,000.

The brainchild of renowned comic editor Shelly Bond and Kristy and Brian Miller of Hi-Fi colour design, Femme Magnifique brings together a frankly incredible cast of creators to celebrate an equally incredible cast of 50 women, 'from astronauts and abolitionists to computer coders and crack journalists.'

'The ERA has never been passed, doesn't that seem weird in a world where a woman can run for President?' questions Kristy. 'Women are still overlooked and treated unfairly in many aspects of life. From receiving a loan to running a company we are still a patriarchal society and women are not treated equally. It is important to show young women that there have been pioneers before you and alongside of you, you can be anything you want, you just may have to fight a little harder.'

How did the project come to be? 'Two events ignited last fall to bring Femme Magnifique from theory to reality,' begins Sally. 'The election results were pivotal as it was certainly a missed opportunity for a female President. And the day after the news sunk in, I saw Róisín Murphy, former frontwoman of Moloko, perform live. It was the crush of the ardent Democratic followers, the thousands rallying the troops to prepare for a woman's march to counter the political malaise and the rapturous concert crowd that danced hard and screamed to the beat. When those two moments crystallized, I knew I had to find a way to contribute to the greater good of equal rights.

'I always tell writers and artists to "pitch me the stories only they can tell." So I was taking my own advice. I reached out to Kristy and Brian Miller of Hi-Fi colour design because they were colleagues and seasoned pros whom I could trust, with a similar goal: Triage! To turn the global political negativity into something positive by celebrating the achievements of women from the past and present via the art form we know and love: comics. To remind everyone that we have the ability to change the future. All Femme. Forward.'

Sally Ride, Michelle Obama, Nina Simone, Beth Ditto, Hillary Clinton, Jane Fonda, Joan of Arc, Carrie Fisher, Ada Lovelace, Bjork — through astronauts, First Ladies, mathematicians, YouTubers, Princess Leias — the project spotlights dozens of incredible women and with the likes of Gail Simone, Marguerite Bennett, Gerard Way, Claire Roe and Kieron Gillen to name a (very) select few, it's packing quality on all counts.

They knew from the off Femme Magnifique would be a big project, and that they could easily find supporters, and so turning to Kickstarter for funding was key. They felt the public would support the project because it would resonate with them.

Brian and Kristy aren't new to crowdfunding, having run Kickstarters and Indiegogos before; they learned a lot from Hi-Fi colour for Comics (the book that they co-wrote). 'It's a ton of work,' notes Kristy. 'You have to have a plan in place before you start. Those 30 days fly by and the more you have ready, the more you have worked out ahead of time the smoother everything runs.'

So, the project is (rightfully, excitingly) funded. Now it's time to make it come to life. 'The process is actually pretty cool,' she explains. 'We are working with writers, pencillers, and colourists from all over the world. Getting to see all of these different styles and meeting all of these different people has been amazing. Sure, there is the actual work of editing, trafficking, etc but in reality it is kinda fun!'

Shelly, Kristy & Brian

The whole thing feels fun, to be honest. They're getting to make a project that so many people are excited about, a project that's important; they're collaborating with creators world-over, and they're celebrating a host of kickass women. There's a lot to enjoy, and when Femme Magnifique publishes later this year, that's likely to shine through even more.

'The best part, for me, has been working with friends like Paige Braddock, Gail Simone and Elsa Charretier,' muses Kristy, 'and then getting to meet (& work with) new people like Megan Hutchinson, Sonny Liew, Maris Wicks just to name a few.'

'Getting to work with so many talented, disparate artists has been so gratifying,' Sally agrees. 'Many of them are old friends like Mark Buckingham, Sanford Greene and Gail Simone who owe me favours (ha ha. JK!). But so many writers and artists are new to me. Whether I've been a fan of their work for a few years, like Lucy Knisley, Maris Wicks and Liz Prince, or met them at conventions, it was a great excuse to see how we'd work together.

'Of course I had to be selective with only fifty slots so I was careful to choose a diverse coterie of people who had something truly inspirational and compelling to impart to the masses. I'm sure it was just as difficult for each writer to chose one particular Femme Magnifique subject but to be honest there was little to no overlap. And that will truly resonate when you see the final book.

'You're in for an unbelievable graphic novel anthology that salutes women in pop, politics, science and the arts and the inimitable art form that is the comic book. It will empower and inspire forever more.'

FACTS (ALTERNATIVE)

(ALTERNATIVE) FACTS

NADINE AISHA JASSAT

Fake   News on the TV.
            This movement
Alternative   Facts on the rise.

Call it what you want,   call it a surprise.
Call it anything but –

    We've got to figure out   what's going on
                it's about replacing
    and you can   trust me that I will
                those who control
    the credible sources   are mine
    the real truth   is mine
                the levels of power
    I'll give the power back   to the real people
    the hard working people
                they will take back this country
    people,   ignored voices   I'm doing this for you
                replacing the establishment
    for the people   that are mine.

Call it what you want,   call it a surprise.
Call it anything but –

    I have it   on good authority
                a corrupt political establishment
    my associates   inform   me
                a new government controlled
    you know,   we know,   what the people   know,   no?
                by you the people

and we're for   every man, we're for all   the men,
not all men,   but we're for   your men,
for our men, for   what about the men,
I'm a man   and I have rights.

Call it what you want,   call it a surprise.
Call it anything but –

Alt-right,   conservatives
family preservatives
did you see   what her husband did?
     They have bled us dry
I know where his birth   certificate's hid
I'm taking back the   white   right
     they have robbed
I'm taking back   control
     they have brought about destruction
totality of diversity
     they don't have your good in mind
I'll cut them   down to size.

Call it what you want,   call it a surprise.
Call it anything but –

     The only thing
what happens   between a man and his wife
is private   healthcare on the rise
     that can stop this corrupt machine
women   are   murderers,
saving their own lives
I'm a man of the people,   if the people are mine
grab 'em by the
freedom   of democracy
pariahs   of society
corrupters   of moral decency
it's not us   who have hypocrisy
it's not us   who make false cries.

Call it what you want,   call it a surprise.
Call it anything but –

                    Is
Nasty Women,   Feminists,
Sluts and Fags   and Terrorists,
Arabs, Mexicans,   Communists,
Scroungers, Stealers,   Socialists,
Muslim Islamic   Islamists,
                    You
Cankers   in   the   worm.

Call it what you want,   call it a surprise.
Call it anything, call it any *thing*, call it anything
but lies.

IT'S FUCKING FREEZING

CELESTE W. CLARK

FEARLESS

SIMON WARD

Yesterday and every day there lived a cheeky little rabbit called Risky, who loved to play deadly games with fate. Her fur was fine and mottled like oil mixed with sand, and her only fear was a dull life. Nothing pleased her more than taunting danger. Not carrots, nor napping. And, for a while, she was free.

Risky lived with a shrew called Bait in an overgrown barn that was covered in brambles and peach clematis. In the middle of that barn, there was a tall fern that cut through the rafters and spread out over the roof. Some nights, Risky would say that the stars were especially bright, then ask the shrew to climb up to the highest branch with her.

Bait was slow to remember his own name and always forgot what happened the last time they scaled the fern. For in the woods near their home there lived an Owl, who was often hungry and never full, and she wet her beak at the sight of whiskers.

To keep Bait distracted, Risky would point at The Plough or The Hunter, and sing to her friend about the nameless ghosts that swam across the sky to bring up the sun. Then, as The Fell Queen neared with open talons against the moon, Risky would yell at Bait to bolt for the undergrowth.

One night, Bait lost his tail, then his belly and then his head.

Sullen days followed, riddled with guilt.

Alone again for the first time since a shadow took her family, Risky left the barn and made a home in a burrow near the motorway. She vowed never to play a game at a friend's expense again, and to only take chances with herself. After all, she'd survived the owl. What reason did she have to stop?

Cars sped past her den all day and she loved to hear their engines growl. She'd sit by the gate to her burrow and kick gooseberries into the road with her wide, hind paws; though she soon grew bored and began to lob stones at car windows, or – whenever they were open – at the drivers' heads. The rocks were too small to hurt the passengers or dent the glass, and Risky's aim was awful, but her skills improved with practice.

The first time she smashed a wing mirror it gave her such a thrill that she moved the game to a high spot on a hill overlooking the motorway. She'd lob the rubble from afar and bounce up and down when lorries swerved, but when she hit a baby in the backseat of a Ford Fiesta she decided to stop. The pebble stuck in the child's ear, and its wail reminded her of Bait.

Now, if that was the end of Risky's games she might have been saved. Alas, it was only the beginning. Part of her knew this, and wanted to stop, but the thought was so faint that she let it die.

The rabbit took to playing a new game in darkness called Test the Lights: when there was no traffic around, she'd stand on the road with her eyes ajar and wait till the headlights of oncoming cars became a flat white wall. Then – as the world was crashing all around her – she'd leap off onto the grass and lay back listening to motors speed off towards Bright City.

Late one evening, she tested the lights of an enormous truck hauling a tanker of sewage. She left it too late to jump and had no choice but to fall back and let the terror ride over her. Its metal innards skimmed her eyelashes and the sound of burning petrol tortured her ears, yet she survived it all, once more.

'It's true,' she said to herself: the universe was on her side.

Watching Risky from the edge of the road was a white fox that went by the name of Mr. Big. He was so impressed by the rabbit's game that he decided to approach her, for he was a risk taker of another sort: a diamond thief and a custard snatcher.

Mr. Big called out to her from the bushes, but the wind ate his voice. Again, he flattered her from the dark, only then she turned and saw his sable eyes.

As he stepped down onto a patch of concrete lit by a lamppost, she studied his scarlet waistcoat and his long, expectant stride.

Here, she thought, was a better game.

'Well, rabbit, I see you're a connoisseur. How'd you like to work for me in Bright City?'

Risky had never been there before, content with her games on the in-between world of the motorway.

'It's too far for me', she said.

The fox grinned.

'With all your style you don't know how to hitch a ride?'

He walked into the woods and returned with logs in his teeth that he laid on the road. Then he dragged three orange cones onto the pile.

'I'm the one who put them there,' said Risky, chasing the fox's tail.

As they waited in silence for a car to stop, Risky stood on the tip of her nails and pushed her nose up to the height of Mr. Big's tummy. She waivered on her perch and struggled to hold her breath, but he didn't show that he noticed – such are the ways of a fox.

When a pickup truck finally slowed, Mr. Big and Risky snuck around its rear and climbed onto the back. They were low and snug beneath its cargo of sacks and rugs, long before the driver skirted Mr. Big's blockage and headed towards the lights.

On the way to the city, he told her about his plan.

'Have you ever tasted diamonds in custard before?'

She shook her head and wiggled her ears.

'No? well, they're the tastiest treat in the entire bleedin' universe, look.'

From his waistcoat, the fox pulled out a hip flask, a tiny bowl and a spoon. He poured a yellow cream dotted with iridescent crystals into the bowl and gave it to Risky.

'What's it do?' she asked.

'Makes you ready for whatever's comin', that's what. I've seen squirrels make badgers cry on the ol' custard-cream, little 'un. An', tell me, have you ever tried to make a badger cry?'

Badgers and foxes were the only critters that Risky hadn't tricked before, and she'd didn't want to make anyone sob, though the custard did look tasty.

As she lifted the gloop to her lips, she began to wonder if she should get out, go home and find a new game on her own. It seemed like the right thing to do, but her urge for a scare was far too great.

She watched her burrow fade away and looked up at the stars. They shone almost as bright as the diamonds in her bowl; the diamonds she drank with the custard.

'In a few minutes, you'll feel bigger than a stag and quicker than a silverfish.'

True enough, Risky felt just that far too soon.

Round and round she paced with a twitch she couldn't place and a dryness in her throat. She didn't know what to do with her energy, so she bounced over to the side of the pickup, opened the latches and kicked off a sack of onions that went under the back wheel.

Mr. Big raised his chin and showed his gums. They were black as death's mirror.

Worried he'd knocked off the exhaust, the driver pulled up on the hard shoulder and exited his car. When he saw the sack and the open latch, he asked his son to get out help him.

With the speed of ten flares, Risky took a bundle of newspapers in her teeth, launched herself sideways into the driver's seat and dropped the stack onto the accelerator. The girl next to her didn't know whether to scream or to smile, so her body leaned towards both reactions, producing a peculiar, terrified grin. The father and his boy tried to catch up, yelling out, though it did them no good, for their pickup was gone.

Risky used her legs to steer, swerving every way imaginable.

Her eyes vibrated towards the edge of their sockets, as though they longed to be free of her head. Drivers banged their horns or skid out the way, sure they were dreaming or dead. And she curved on like that for a mile, scorching tarmac, until the truck slowed on its last drip of gas and came to an appalling, skewed halt.

Sirens approached yet Risky couldn't let go of the wheel because her heart was trying to abandon her chest. The young girl whined and stroked her seatbelt.

Ahead was Bright City, and the smog that bled out its lights.

Mr. Big opened the door and watched Risky from the road. She didn't notice he was there.

'You've done well, very well. How's about you get down before The Fat Men come?'

'I don't feel good, not good at all.'

'You're just burnt out. Come on, have another spoon.'

'Spoon?'

'Custard, darlin'. You're on the custard now.'

That night, they would take on the biggest purveyor of shiny goo in the world, and steal from the house of Ol' Madam Scales.

Risky didn't know who The Madam was or what it meant to steal from her. Either way, she didn't care. Her mind was set on diamonds and, in that moment, nothing else mattered.

As the white fox lead Risky through the city towards the Madam's home, life seemed strange and beautifully dangerous. Rats dived in gutters, humans wailed in the distance and every so often, far away, something smashed. The buildings were huge and faceless though lights popped up all over their walls like ticks. And, every time Risky and the fox turned a corner, they had to hide.

Onwards they went, through parks, past pubs and along a canal, until they reached the outskirts of Bright City: the woods that cut off the rich from the poor.

Within that forest was The Madam's estate. It was boarded up with steel bars, locked in by a great wall and guarded by ruthless hounds, though Mr. Big knew a way inside.

To lead the dogs astray, he covered himself and Risky in an anti-smell spray that he kept in the lining of his waistcoat. Then he walked into the woods and came back with several sacks of cat pee that he threw into the bushes within the estate, launching them at different spots around the enclosure.

Whilst the dogs ran in loops looking for the bags, Mr. Big gave Risky another spoon and told her to squeeze through a gap under the gate, promising her that he wasn't far behind.

Pushed on by the custard, she skulked across the garden towards the manor.

The grass was sharp and moist. It smelt acrid and synthetic.

Once Risky reached the red-brick walls, she climbed up a drainpipe and slipped through an open window, landing on a velvet carpet.

The lights were red and the walls were bronze.

In the middle of the room, there was a monstrous safe with a combination lock. Mr. Big came up behind her and fiddled with its dial until it clicked. It seemed odd that it gave way so easily, but Risky was too excited to question what was going on − seconds were passing ten-thousand times their normal speed.

Inside the safe, there was a gold bowl encrusted with diamonds and filled with custard. Mr. Big told her to grab it and to bring it to him without spilling any, so she edged forward and lifted the prize from its ivory table.

As it slid into her paws, a harsh bell rang and a fluorescent-yellow spray shot out to stain her fur. Mr. Big grabbed the custard, glugged the liquid and run out the room.

By the time she knew what had happened, the fox was long gone.

Short of breath and wild, Risky went for the window. The floor spun at her feet and her teeth ground of their own accord. She started to feel sluggish and far too tired to think. That's when the door behind her creaked and flung open.

Stood there in the hallway was Madam Scales: a grey lioness in a navy-blue suit with a steel whistle around her neck. In her paw was an old-fashioned rifle and at her waist was a long truncheon. She aimed the gun at Risky, took a shot and shattered a vase. That was enough to force the rabbit up the ledge, out of the window and into the bushes below.

Risky was slow to fight her way out of the thorns and her anti-smell spray was wearing off. The dogs sniffed the air and drew back into a pack. They saw Risky from afar, and she saw them; never had she felt so alone, and never had she been so scared.

She fled to the gate with her sight on the gap but turned at the sound of a whistle. The dogs slowed on the grass and sat in a line with their spines straight. She could almost hear their breath. They seemed to look right through her.

Down from the manor came a cream Rolls-Royce and behind its wheel was Madam Scales. She let the engine moan, turned on the headlights and came down the driveway.

Risky didn't move, she couldn't, because her feet were stuck to the path.

Mr. Big watched her through the bars. There was a slim trail of glue that led from his feet to her own, and a brush in his right paw. He placed it on the floor, lowered his head and stepped backwards – lost to the night forever.

The Madam drove up slowly, opened the door and brought out a cage. She walked up to Risky, bent over her and clenched her ears.

There was too much fear in the rabbit to let her tears flow, so her eyes became glossy pearls; and, as she booted the air, she bit her own lip.

It was a small key for a small abode. The bars were tight, unbreakable and cold.

Fallen leaves turned into snow and spring came back again. Those months became years. Risky watched them pass behind steel, sat at the back of The Madam's garden upon a pile of bricks.

She was let out once a day for an hour to play, within an enclosed pen upon a lead, under the glare of the hounds – who watched her sleep and snarled when she sang. Some days, she heard them talk, but they never spoke to her, and, once, they mentioned the fox.

Her food was dry, her life was quiet and she often drank rain.

For the first time in her life, Risky lost the game.

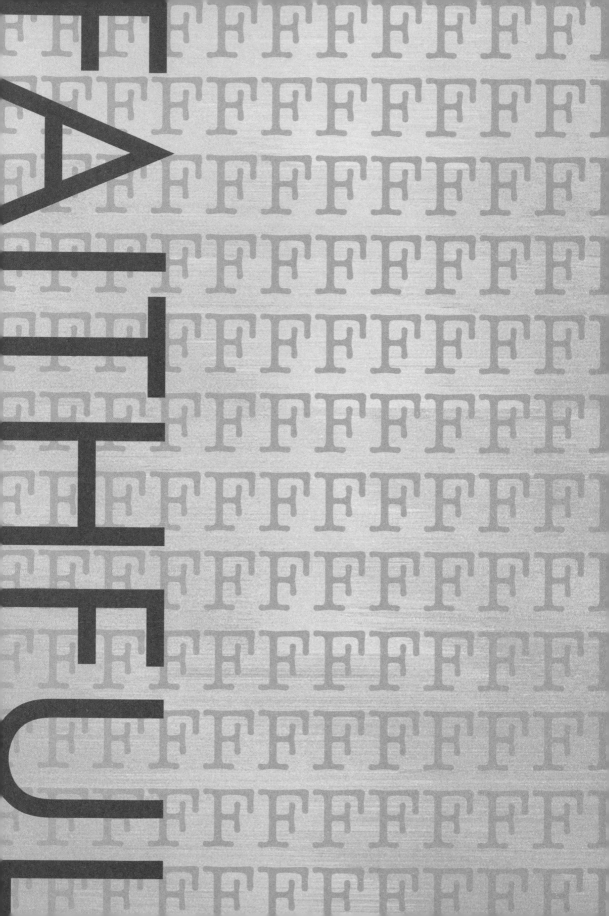

FAITHFUL

FAITHFUL

TOM-PAUL SMITH

new year's eve

Sometime before midnight he walks out onto a balcony. He climbs onto the ledge and stands there – on the tails of an old year, inching precariously toward the new. He spots me below, on the other side of the street. He stops. It has been raining all night and the road holds reflections of the city skyline on the ground, like a dazzling kaleidoscopic painting on a wet canvas. Water drips into the drains, reflecting lights like electric fire. He climbs off the ledge; his eyes remain fixed on me. He smiles, but looks embarrassed. Across the road from me, he is two floors up from a tree-lined boulevard. He disappears back into his apartment. I return my attention to the street again. Most of the snow has melted during the day and now a glossy sheen covers the roads. A small group of revellers come into view, giggling and swigging drinks. They kick and throw what's left of the snow at one another. Later on it becomes busy. People are rushing hither-thither, I guess from one party to another, before the midnight hour strikes. He has returned to the balcony, now brandishing a flute of champagne in his hand. As the clock strikes midnight I hear cheering from the cafes and bars. He raises his glass to me and mouths 'Happy New Year'. Somewhere fireworks go off. I watch their dazzling colours reflecting in the apartment windows in front of me. I scan from window to window, stealing delight from celebrations never intended for me. He remains out in the cold for another hour or so before waving goodbye and returning to his apartment.

spring

Life has returned. People on the street look fresh and rested from their winter hibernation. It's as if they too are sprouting the first shoots of optimism for what the year has in store.

One hazy morning I am forced forward with a violent strike. I'm stripped. My clothes torn away with impatient hands. An overweight woman huffs and puffs as she picks up my scattered clothes from the floor. She leaves. I'm left naked. A few people in the street notice me, but no one cares about a department mannequin having her dignity stolen. Later that morning a young store assistant walks over to me. With gentle hands, she slips my arms into a white crepe shirt. The two top buttons left undone. With care, she lowers me onto the worn carpet to get a pair of tights on me. This is something she hasn't got the knack of. It takes her a long while to get them on; she has to wiggle my feet about to get them over my heels. It gives me a chance to look around the store. The other models are poorly made and some are downright grotesques – missing limbs and decapitated bodies. I try not to judge, but some of the clothes they wear – good heavens! None of their outfits matches. Once I am back upright she pulls a knee-length blue pencil skirt around my waist. The outfit is complete with a matching blazer. It's a business suit! I feel its power and authority hum through my plastic body. Before the young woman leaves she repositions my arms. I now stand with authority, arms folded across my chest. The ruthless stance of the modern business age.

He says he wants to be my boyfriend. He tells me he loves me. Maybe he does. In the evenings I usually see him. When he walks down the street he looks happy. He once told me this is his favourite moment of the day. I want to be a good girlfriend, so it is my favourite moment of the day also. When he first came into the store he was nervous. It was only a couple of days into the new year. I didn't recognise him at first. On a meandering journey towards my window he stopped several times. He pretended to look at clothes on a rack, or to look at his watch. When he stood by my side he introduced himself, almost in a whisper. He often glanced around the store and touched his face when he spoke. He told me he felt the need to explain his actions from New Year's Eve. He said it had been six months since he last spoke to Maria, his ex-girlfriend; we don't like her or her new boyfriend Kenny. He tells me they had been through difficult times before, and assumed they would get through this one. They had a good social life, both together and separately. Then one night she left without warning. She phoned him two days later to explain that she'd met someone else. My boyfriend imagined Maria and her new boyfriend celebrating New Year's Eve together. Maybe on some exotic beach – drinking fluorescent cocktails and giggling under a warm sun. He said that night in his apartment he could hear their laughter echoing around his head. He said he would never have gone through with jumping. He tells me he is dependable.

summer

The endless days and humid nights can mean only one thing: summer has finally arrived. It warms the street, igniting the weeds and grasses that grow in the cracked pavement.

Customers now fill the store daily. They rush about, caught up in the heat and frenzy of the long days. Gone is my business attire. The young assistant has given me a beautiful cotton dress and matching sandals. My legs feel the warmth of the morning sun shining through the store window. I also have a new posture! It's the pose of someone who should be carefree and ready to embrace the world – a hand on my hips, one arm flying in the air and a twist in my waist. The dress and happy-go-lucky demeanour do have their downsides. The men on the street, when they look at me they seem to think about what it would be like to go to bed with me. I can tell this not by the way they leer at my breasts and hips and partially exposed legs, but by the way they try not to as they walk past the window.

My boyfriend never leers. When he tells me he loves me I can see happiness in his face. There is no reply. My lips do not move. My face remains static. None of this matters. For the first time he visits me during the workday. He should be in the office, but he is ill. He suffers from hay-fever and has taken two days off. He comments on my new dress, he likes my new look. My boyfriend has more confidence now. He no longer appears awkward. He stands up straight and says 'I got you this.' He puts a thin silver bracelet on my wrist and beams. When he leaves I hear the women from the department store snigger. They call my boyfriend a 'weirdo' and an 'oddball.' He sometimes talks about all the little things Maria said that upset him. He has a long list. I think this is why I appeal to him. Outside in his world, people's responses are unpredictable, frightening or demeaning. The wrong reactions seem to upset my boyfriend. I give him a predictable comfort; I have never said an unkind word to him. I cannot offend him by being aloof or giving him an upsetting look. Our relationship is sterile but clean and free from the usual strains.

autumn

As the nights grow darker and the last of the summer fruits have been eaten, we welcome autumn. Leaves lay glossy on the rain-washed street.

I have a seductive bedroom look. A sensual bodysuit with a scrappy open front and keyhole crisscross-lacing back. It's made to thrill, with a bold red robe. My hand has been placed across the top of my chest with the other resting by my side. It is a beautiful pose to bring out my desirability and femininity.

My boyfriend is taken aback the first time he sees my new look. He is nervous at first, like the first time we met in the store. After a few more visits he changes. When he feels no one in the store is looking he tenderly strokes my leg. Sometimes he holds my hand as he tells me about his day. His palms are always sweaty. He is thoughtful. He is always asking me questions like, 'Are you warm enough?' He never looks at the other mannequins as he walks over. His passionate eyes are always fixed on mine. Does it matter if I'm not real? It doesn't matter to my boyfriend. When a man stares at a naked woman, is it really her personality he is interested in? Is a woman's personality not the thing that some men wish to escape from? One time his phone rang while we were together. He pulled it out and scoffed at it. 'Now she calls, when I'm finally happy again.' He hung up and replaced the phone back into his jacket. I heard today he might be going to Hong Kong next month for a business trip. 'It's up in the air right now, but if it does happen I'll bring you back something nice.' His gaze goes down my body before he looks back up at me and caresses my cheek. 'It'll only be for a week... Absolutely not, work only. I have no intention of visiting those places.'

winter

The bitter wind outside reminds us that winter is approaching fast. I observe frost glistening on the pavement in the morning half-light. Within the apartment block across the road are every child's Christmas dreams.

A new store assistant dresses me. She is middle-aged and has a large face with plump lips, and a thick mask of makeup. She handles me firmly, but not with malice. She turns around as she removes my lingerie. I inspect the other models – they've not had a good year. Most have cracks in their skin, all have scraggly hair. When the assistant is finished I am back staring out of the window. I'm wearing a beautiful vintage-inspired mint-green winter coat – the perfect antidote to any winter blues. It is made from luxurious, soft materials with a detachable hood and faux fur trim to keep in much-needed heat during these months. She has even teamed my outfit with a pair of matching gloves and a cosy knitted scarf.

Snow begins to fall. I watch as cascading flakes dance on the wind. My boyfriend is walking down the street; plumes of his breath rise into the slate-grey sky. I see him approaching behind me in the reflection of the store window. Once inside he stops and watches the street outside with me. In the reflection we look like a washed out photograph. When he does turn to face me he still has snowflakes in his hair. He tells me he likes my new coat and says I look 'homely'. Then he explains that he turned down his business trip because he couldn't be away from me. The way my boyfriend looks at me tells me I should be happy, so I am happy. He reminds me it's been almost a year since we first met. He tells me he has a special question to ask me tomorrow. My boyfriend looks excited.

At night, when the store is closed to customers, the middle-aged store assistant is talking to some men. I hear them say I am to be relocated to a new flagship store in a big city. I take a last look across at my boyfriend's apartment. I guess I am also capable of betrayal. I wonder what he wanted to ask me tomorrow. I'm escorted to a van. As I am driven away into the winter night I guess we'll see how much he really does love me, as he said he does.

UNDER HER SKIRTS
SHE IS WILD WITH
JUST THE TRACE
OF FEAR

UNDER HER SKIRTS SHE IS WILD WITH JUST THE TRACE OF EARTH

HANNAH LAVERY

The house is still in its winter gloom. Not ready for spring. Still it's time for the tulips.

He will be chuffed to come home to them, all their dangling heads. Now that's a rare thing he'll say but it breaks her heart to see the way the house devours them. To watch them so fresh from the bed to over days bow out in front of her. She feels a traitor to something, pulling them up. Gathering them all dead wee toy soldiers in her grandmother's trug.

He's a tyrant of planned borders and his yearning for perfection, a suffocating fog. She snips away at the red and yellow thinking he wasn't always this way, remembers his old wild abandon, those earlier eyes of his and for a moment she is famished but she does her job quickly. Then heads straight up to the top of the garden, by the shed and the compost.

She dug a patch here last summer ready for vegetables but she has planted nothing yet. A poor job on her part he said but she only smiled and said tomorrow. Then tomorrow and then again tomorrow and then her tomorrow became winter. Now spring but still the patch of mud is a patch of mud.

She stands at the edge of her barren plot unsure. The unsure pricking, tugging, exciting, befuddling and then caught in it. Caught. She quickly removes her coat. Then slowly, deliberately, she takes off her gloves. Her shoes. Her socks. Unzips and rolls down her jeans. Removes her knickers. Throws off her sweatshirt. Strips off her vest. Unclips and frees herself of her bra. Naked she grabs the spade that stands watchman against their bent out fence. She starts to dig. Her body soon becomes goosebumped. Her nipples hard. Sweat rolls gathering like rainwater in the small in her back.

And the neighbours. Those onlookers from all sides start picking up their phones. Exclaiming outrage and fake concern on Facebook. Husbands are being called home.

She continues to dig. And dig. And dig. Creating a dark hole and feeling the hundred what the... She lowers herself down inside, into that dark damp soil thinking this is exactly where I should be. She fixes on the tiny threads of roots in her mud walls, on the worms and hair thin spiders. She knows he will soon be home. That he will drag her out by her hair. Apologies to neighbours will need to be made. The hole filled. But for now it's a long way off. Time now to dream. Naked. Mud encrusted. Sweat running in her cracks and crevices. Blissed out in all her sea salt sea.

FUCKING

FANCY DRESS

FUCKING FANCY DRESS

CLAIRE SQUIRES

We get a scrawled invitation, late, from number four. Come round, it's going to be fun. They must have forgotten they had neighbours, and that we wouldn't be asleep anyway, and that we wouldn't mind the noise. It's one of those parties, the letter parties, where you choose a letter of the alphabet and you have to go round in fancy dress as that letter. It's someone's birthday next door – Frank, is it? Fred? I forget. Anyway, we fucking hate fancy dress. I've got a flapper dress but I don't want to wear it, too much of a cliché. We dig out old costumes from former parties. We remember that famous time I went to Hallowe'en party as a jar of Marmite. Fucking frightening, someone said. You said, Can I lick you? I fucking love Marmite, mmm, mmm, ffff.

It's the kind of night where a quick brown fox might jump, if it felt like it, over the lazy dog next door. Just for the fun of it. We're feeling lazy, it's that kind of summer's evening. We're filled with energy, for the night ahead. It feels like it's already only beginning, it's late but the sun is still high.

It's high summer, the garden is in full bloom. We take a beer and head out of the French windows. It's lush, the foliage. It was raining for a couple of weeks, but then the sun came full on, and it's been growing and growing, a forest. Fur winds around our ankles, the cat yowling for her food.

Over the fence we can hear the noise of the party. We could just go as Adam and Eve, after the serpent though, fig leaves covering us. Or flowers in our hair, Woodstock style. Or some other festival; Glastonbury. Fritillaries. Foxgloves. Forget-me-nots. Freesias…the fragrance.

We haven't had enough to drink yet for full exposure. I grab the dictionary off the shelf and flip through it. Some pages float free from the dictionary. It's illustrated, full of pictures of fawns, and fronds, and Fibonacci sequences. The air fills with words, flying with ideas, floating around our heads.

We go round to number four and Fungus the Bogeyman lets us in. A couple of fanatics or fucking hipsters or something nod at us in the hallway. We head to the kitchen and stash our beer in the fridge, then out into the garden. There's a firefighter with a girl over his shoulder. Someone is playing a fiddle. People are sticking their heads through a frame; kissing from each side. At one end of the garden they're talking politics, fear and fury, it's a free world. Someone says each summer party is a tiny fiefdom. Others are juggling words up in to the air, doing free association. One of them throws back her head and says something about Freud.

I hear a filthy laugh; and a whisper of fellatio. I see you flirting with a battered fish; I chat up chips.

I fucking hate fancy dress.

A few stars appear in the sky. I shiver and go to the fire. Someone puts a glass of Fitou in my hand. Foutu is French for fucked. Fingers brush mine.

I feel unsteady on my feet. Fault lines open.

The neighbour's dog runs from the undergrowth at the bottom of the garden. I smell the scent of fox.

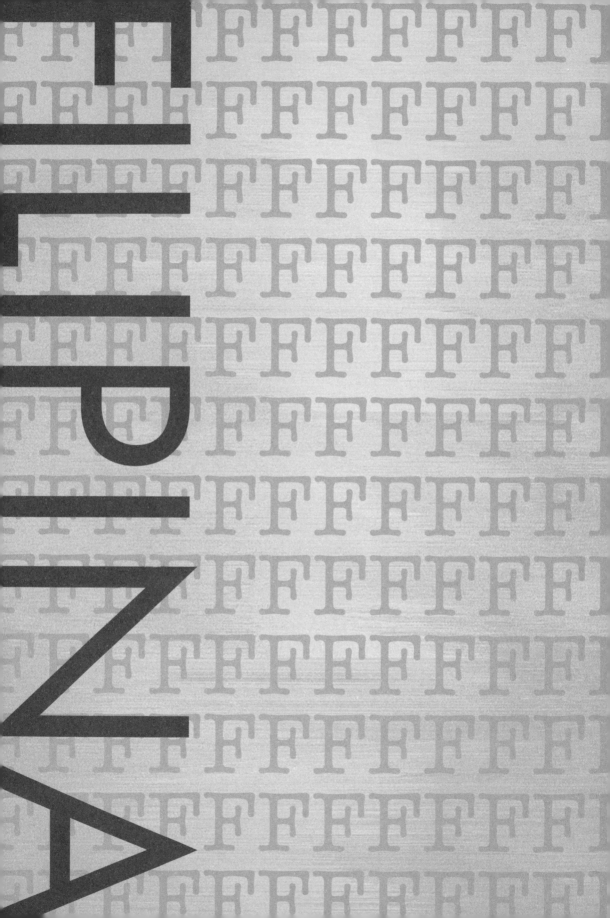

FILIPINA

FILIPINA
RIA CAGAMPANG

I have long fought the colour of my skin
Itched
Scratched at the other
Hidden under
white, translucent, creams, powders
A chemical mask is easy to peel on and off
when your existence feels poisonous to the majority

But my yellow undertones are
no longer so hidden under tones
Hushed, no more
Today, I erase, no more
I, no longer Mestiza
I, no longer model minority
I, no longer compliant.
No longer pliant to the will of the majority

I *thrive* off my ancestry
They, not pliant to the will of the majority
My passion for words rises, guttural
Tinged with the legacy of Rizal on my white washed shoulders
I survive by the sacrifices made by warriors, rebel soldiers and tribal priestesses
Maria, atop Makiling
I arise in the shadow of your towering form

Now
Hear me fight
for the colour of my skin

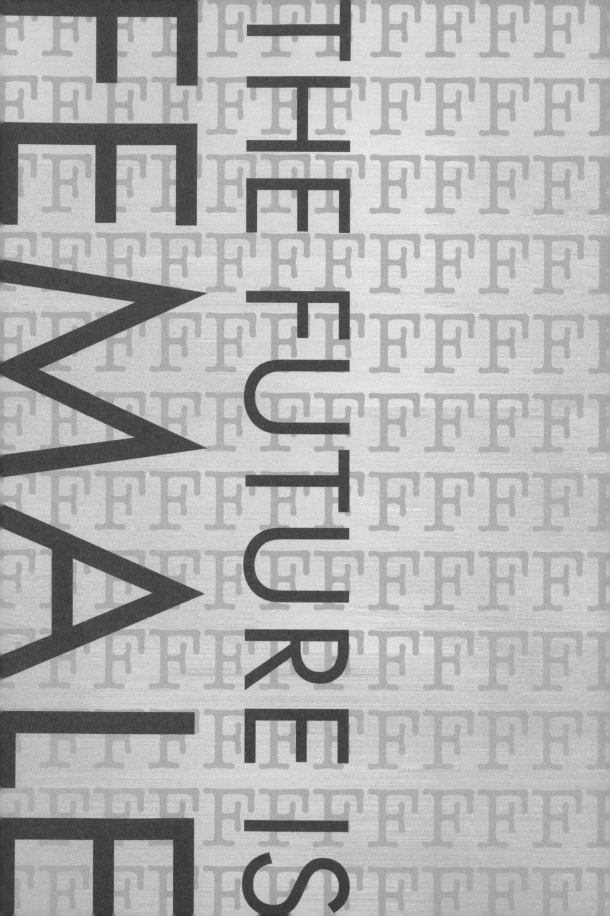

THE FUTURE IS FEMALE

THE FUTURE IS FEMALE

KATY LENNON

IN THE ROBOTIC LAW COURT IN EDINBURGH
Witness: Cassidy, Lena
IN THE MATTER OF LAW(S) OF SUBSERVIENCE NO. 1, 2 AND 3
(running OS 101.9)
Statement no. 097652
Case no. 99
STATEMENT AS FOLLOWS

I walked off the stage and into the arms of my PA. She was shoving a towel in my face, drying off the sweat while simultaneously trying not to ruin my makeup. I grabbed it from her. 'It's not like it matters now! They've had their fill.' I let the colours bleed together, the sting of sweat and mascara in my eyes. She stared at me. I must have looked a total mess. I laughed as I went into my dressing room.

I couldn't have been sitting down for more than five minutes before another assistant walked in (without knocking), reminding me without even looking up that we needed to rehearse for the second show the following night. I was exhausted, but at her command stripped off my performance costume and got into some comfortable rehearsal clothes. Another assistant entered and I asked if I could go see my girls, sign some autographs while they were setting up for rehearsal; sweeping up confetti, sluicing down the stage for sweat and spit. They said no. I sat and waited. Another five minutes. Another assistant.

Rehearsals are always easy, I don't know why we still do them. I only have two albums out; the first one is so familiar to me now I could do it in my sleep, the second one was the high pressure sell, so I had to do a million live performances. Morning shows, lunchtime shows, late night shows, online exclusives, live performances, New Year's Eve… my point is I fucking know it. But I went through the dance moves, the routines, leaning on or caressing dancers who weren't there, the little winks, and sexy looks into camera one, camera three, camera eight. I had it down. I clicked my limbs into place, my hips rotated at perfect angles. The only word to describe my dancing is mathematic. I can calculate my movements down to the millimetre.

Suddenly I can't move my torso. It feels like I've pulled every muscle in my body. And there's a squealing sound which I think is a girl screaming but what turns out to be one of the bars from the rigging twisting downwards and into my stomach. Instinctively my hands move to the wound, ready to catch the presumed blood that would soon be gushing out. But my hands were dry. And there was no screaming. Some expressed notes of frustration, some even stretched to a small cry of surprise. But no screams. I noticed I wasn't screaming either. People scream when I walk into a room, but now….but now…but now…

They were gathering around me with bored, impatient expressions on their faces. It seemed like this had happened before. Like when the internet cuts out and you have to reset the router. They grabbed me roughly with bored hands. Their nails pinched. It was late. They all wanted to get home, and this was the last thing they had to do before they could clock off. They pulled it out front-ways, so I could see it, and it was impossible for me to do anything. It came out clean save for a few sparks and occasional cavernous cracks, spreading like a scar across the empty stadium. They were treating me like a piece of the stage. Like a broken mic stand, I was to be patiently, grudgingly repaired and cleaned up for use, until the next time I inevitably failed, and relied on them to show me how to dance for them again, how to gyrate at 5AM every day, how to sit quietly in a dressing room and how to do as I'm told. I moved my eyes to my right hand. The finger twitched. I don't remember what happened after that. Look, that's all I remember, now where is my tech manager? We've got a fucking show to do.

TO THE BEST OF MY MEMORY, THE FACTS STATED ARE TRUE
IN THE ROBOTIC LAW COURT IN EDINBURGH
Witness: Model 0997
IN THE MATTER OF LAW(S) OF SUBSERVIENCE NO. 1, 2 AND 3
(running OS 66.0)
Statement no. 097653
Case no. 99
STATEMENT AS FOLLOWS

I was reorganizing Ms Urbach's schedule. She entered the room just as I reached next Thursday evening. She was talking out loud, but was alone. I recorded her dialogue as I was the default addressee. Audio transcript was as follows.

'Fucking useless, incompetent ingrates, don't they realize everything I've done for them? Can't even depend on the ones you RAISED YOURSELF to defend you when your ass is on the line. Well, I know who'll be coming with me to start my competitor company. I'm going to tear these girls' guts out, I swear…'

Any further dialogue was unable to be processed by my language categorization systems. I didn't receive any commands, so I took no further action. Ms Urbach stared at me, so I retraced the dialogue just in case I had missed my wake word. INCOMPETENT ingrates, ASS on the line, tear these girls' GUTS OUT… Ms Urbach raised her voice when she spoke to me next. 'WELL?! Where the fuck is my fucking drink?! Can't any of you people take a hint? Or do I have to spell everything out for you?' I went to the bar to mix Ms Urbach's martini. Ms Urbach was pacing back and forth. Once I had made the martini, I brought it to her desk. 'I suppose you aren't even going to ask me how it went.' I took this as a hint.

'How did the meeting go, Ms Urbach?' I asked. She rolled her eyes at me. 'Fucking fantastic! They want me to take over the company! How do you think it went, you useless thing? They're cutting me out! Cutting me out of my own deal! I was the one out there shaking hands and signing contracts, and now they're telling me I'm not a valuable asset. There's no respect, no integrity left in this industry anymore.' I wasn't sure how to respond to this. Ms Urbach had not touched her drink. I moved it closer to her, and initiated my sympathy protocol.

'There, there. Everything is going to be alright. I'm sure tha…' I could not finish as Ms Urbach had picked up the glass and thrown it at me. I tasted gin. 'Don't you dare give me any of that useless pre-programmed sympathy card bullshit! I'm so fucking sick of listening to your empty chatter day in, day out. It means NOTHING, do you hear me? Everything that comes out of that pretty mouth of yours means NOTHING! So don't even bother.'

I was having trouble understanding this. I wasn't sure what response to employ. 'You haven't even considered this, have you? That you're just a toy for us, something to make us feel better. And most of the time you can't even do that properly. You're a glorified sex toy, a game we play while waiting for the internet to load. So just shut the fuck up, do what you're supposed to do, and make me another martini.'

It was at this point I lost control of my motor functions. I began accepting dialogue prompts I didn't recognize. From this point onwards all audio/visual recording was lost, except three files. SOUNDBITE: RECOGNIZED. FILE UNDER: SHATTERING GLASS. Audio output, origin Unit 0997: 'SHUT THE FUCK UP! SHUT THE FUCK UP! SHUT THE FUCK UP!'

TO THE BEST OF MY MEMORY, THE FACTS STATED ARE TRUE
IN THE ROBOTIC LAW COURT IN EDINBURGH
Witness: Model 1009 (MOLLY)
IN THE MATTER OF LAW(S) OF SUBSERVIENCE NO. 1, 2 AND 3
(running OS 90.10)

Statement no. 097654
Case no. 99
STATEMENT AS FOLLOWS

I like it when Dodd isn't home. I can clean her work clothes, and watch the blood and grime swirl down the drain. I always think every fresh set of clothes I wash could be taking her one step closer to retirement. So somehow I convince myself that if I could only wash enough clothes I could get her there. She works so hard. And all she wants to do is earn enough money to stop the dirty work and settle down. Marry me. She always talks about our kids, how they'd be sweet like me and salty like her. That always makes me think of popcorn. And I think of them, waiting in some pod somewhere, waiting for us to be ready for them, like how the one packet of food or that one piece of clothing you were always destined to pick sits and waits for you? Until you come along and make it yours. You know what I mean? Never mind.

I was doing the laundry, playing house, pretending like no-one was home, even though Dodd's friends were smoking joints in the living room. I hate when they do that, it stinks the place up. Dodd always laughs at me for complaining, says the place stinks as it is, might as well make it stink of something that smells good. I wasn't expecting her home for a few hours at least, but just as I was hanging up the last of the clean white shirts to dry, I heard the door, and Dodd's voice fill the living room. I forced the last shirt onto the drying rack and ran through the house in my bare feet. When I opened the door the sunlight ripped through my nightgown. It's retro, from the sixties. Pink. Girls back then would wear like three layers of underwear under something like this. I was wearing panties.

Dodd always looks at me like I'm the most beautiful thing in the world when she gets home from a hard day's work. In those moments I think I can feel myself glowing. I'm in her lap, and she's already pulling at the pink silk ribbon around my neck before she tells the girls to get out. They grumbled, one snatching up one of the ashtrays from the windowsill, smoke drifting up from her mouth. I don't recognize her. Dodd's hand slips inside my nightgown and she has one of my tits in her mouth before the grumbly one has left the room. She turns away quickly. I laughed loud. Dodd likes it when I laugh. Then I let out a yelp as Dodd's teeth closed over my nipple.

'Hey! Be gentle!' before the words are even out of my mouth I'm on the floor, all the air forced out of my lungs. 'I'll be gentle when I wanna be fuckin' gentle, bitch' she growls, already bored, lighting another cigarette. 'and I'll be rough whenever I wanna be rough.' She flicked a switchblade out of her jeans pocket and it toyed with the light glinting off it and up across the walls. 'Yeah, I know baby. It's all you. I got it. It just hurt is all!' Dodd walked slowly over before crouching down next to me. The knife is catching on the cheap nylon of my nightgown. The fabric is so cheap it frays immediately. 'You're gonna ruin my nightdress baby…I know how much you like this one…come on, I can make you feel better…' I put my arms around her neck.

'No. I'm bored of that now. I wanna see what else I can do to you.' A burst of heat along my jawline as she takes the knife to my face. I feel her hands between my legs. 'Let's just make it a little more interesting…I wanna see how far you can go for me.' I whimper without consent, and the girls let out a low collection of knowing laughs. 'Please baby, I don't want this right now. I'm not turned on, okay?! Stop! It really hurts!' But she disabled any defensive motor functions the day she brought me home; I just lie there and take it. She drags the knife across my body, shaving hair, removing layers of skin, making tiny mouths of flesh with the lips puckered to kiss. It disappears, reappears. I feel like I'm on fire. I beg her to stop. She keeps going, taking little pieces of me off, seeing how far she can drive it in. Playing with me. I just keep repeating; stop, stop STOP! The large glass ashtray sitting on the table is in my hand then split across Dodd's head, blood pouring immediately, the bright red making my pupils vibrate. But there are more heavy things in the room and they all come crashing down on her skull, again again again again until I can be sure, until I know she'll stop. I take the clean knife from Dodd's hand just as the door swings open. My wounds seal themselves and I stand naked and drenched in sunlight. The new girl's joint falls from mouth to floor.

TO THE BEST OF MY MEMORY, THE FACTS STATED ARE TRUE
PRESIDING OFFICER'S COMMENTS

These statements were taken from all three AI units on the 16th of February 2029. Due to the special circumstances of murder as well as breakages of all three Laws of Subservience all three fembots were decommissioned soon afterwards, on the 20th of February 2029. This case proved to be the last straw in addressing the unquestioned presence of fembots in the lives of women and girls the world over. The story of the murdered people and the three rogue fembots spread, and now almost all of them have been placed in sanctioned safe zoned, with several thousand awaiting decommission. This case has been filed as closed.

Officer Freya Malmstedt

A FISTFUL OF COPPERS

CHRIS MCQUEER

'I can't go to school. She'll hit me again, Mum,' Carly whined. Her bottom lip quivered. She was talking about Chantelle at school. A big brute of a lassie who had been giving wee Carly grief. She slagged her for the fact she got her shoes from Brantano, for the fact her mum didn't have a car and for anything else really that Chantelle could think of. She especially liked calling her "Clatty Carly". Chantelle was a right wee cow.

'Well if she tries anything the day while am there,' Carly's maw, Julie, said, 'there'll be three hits; me hitting her, her hitting the deck and then the ambulance hitting ninety.'

Julie was heading straight to work after dropping Carly off and she checked her purse for bus fare. No change. Bastard. She rooted around in her hand bag – there must be some change in there. She emptied the bag and turned it upside down – nothing. Julie realised she was going to have to raid the wee jar full of coppers. *Dropping two quid's worth of coppers into the wee hing in front ae a bus full a people – what a fucking riddy*, she thought. She put the change into her purse and tried to zip it up but failed.

Walking through the fine drizzly rain to school, Carly was deathly quiet. The thought of what Chantelle would do to her today terrified her. She had visions of Chantelle grabbing her maw and tombstoning her down into the ground before turning round and punching Carly so hard her head came flying clean off her shoulders and into orbit. Carly thought she was going to be sick.

'Hurry up, hen,' Julie shouted back at her daughter. As they approached the school gates, Julie watched Chantelle's maw drive away in her Range Rover. Julie felt her hand curl up into a tight fist. Her nails dug into her palm. 'Snobby cow,' she muttered under her breath.

'Who is?' Carly asked. Julie hadn't realised she'd caught up with her. 'Eh, naebody, sweetheart. I didnae say anyhin.' Carly hid behind her mother as the playground came into view. Chantelle stood leaning against a wall, watching her. She spat on the ground. Carly grabbed the bottom of her Julie's jacket.

'Please just let me stay off. Please, mum?' she begged.

'Am sorry, Carly doll. Ye cannae. I've got to go to work. Just go in there and play wi yer wee pals and I'll wait here until the bell goes, awrite?'

Carly reluctantly edged into the playground, hoping Chantelle wouldn't see her. She had no such luck. Chantelle blocked Carly's path as she went to join her pals. She circled round her. Carly felt like a gazelle being stalked by a lion in the documentaries watched sometimes. She remembered it never ended well for the gazelle. Chantelle pushed her from behind and Carly went down face first into a puddle. Chantelle stamped an Ugg boot-clad foot down into the puddle, sending a mini tsunami crashing over Carly's face and walked away. Carly got to her feet and ran back to her maw.

Julie tried to contain her rage towards this wee horror of a lassie that had just decked her daughter. She wanted to storm into the playground and drop-kick the wee bitch. She was about to do just that – then she had an idea. She dried her daughter's face with her jumper and took her hand.

'Here, hen,' she said to Carly. She grabbed as much change from her purse as she could and poured the coins into Carly's hand.

'I don't want money, mum, I want to go home,' Carly said, wiping tears away from her eyes.

'Yer no gawn hame. Yer gonnae give that lassie a piece ae yer mind. Make a fist.'

'Like this?' Carly struggled to close her hand right over but it was a definite fist. She struggled to lift her hand up from her side due to the weight of the coins. Julie checked her watch; the bell was due to ring any second now.

'Aye, just like that. Now and go and skelp her. She'll no be messing wi ye anymore after this, pal.'

Carly walked over to Chantelle. She had returned to her spot leaning against the wall – keeping an eye on her prey. She saw Carly striding towards her and a smirk grew across her face, like ivy climbing up a wall.

'Clatty Carly, Clatty Carly, you gonnae run greeting to yer mammy again? Hahahaha,' Chantelle laughed in Carly's face.

Carly let her hand swing back and forth like a pendulum as she came nose-to- nose with Chantelle. The rain was easing off now and the sun was trying its hardest to break through the thick carpet of cloud. Pockets of blue sky appeared here and there. Carly swung her hand back and dropped her shoulder. Her fist came round in a wide circle. Chantelle didn't see it coming until it was too late for her to react. Carly gritted her teeth and let the momentum hurtle her fist into Chantelle's jaw. The full weight of £1.65 in one and two pence pieces crashed into the side of Chantelle's face like a meteorite. Carly kept driving her fist up the way, twisting it as it made impact. The shinier coins glinted in the sunlight as they sprung loose from Carly's hand. Chantelle's head almost spun round 360 degrees like in a cartoon and she hit the deck as the bell rang.

HINGS
by CHRIS MCQUEER

That was a story from Chris McQueer's debut short story collection *Hings*, published in July 2017, from 404 Ink.

'Hilariously surreal snapshots of working class Scotland. Limmy meets Irvine Welsh.' **– Ewan Denny, Link & Lorne**

If you can't wait for that there is a three story e-book preview available at 404ink.com/shop for just £3.

Keep your eye on *404ink.com/chris-mqueer* for information on how you can get your hands on the highly anticipated collection from 'That Guy Oan Twitter Who Writes Short Stories'. (We also heartily recommend you do check him out on Twitter, the guy's a bit hilarious – @ChrisMcQueer)

FORAGING AND FEMINISM

FORAGING AND FEMINISM: HEDGE-WITCHCRAFT IN THE 21ST CENTURY

ALICE TARBUCK

I am in the kitchen, counting out rosehips. It is dark outside, and my partner and I keep forgetting ourselves with cross words. It is early December, but already the star in the window is shedding glitter onto the windowsill. On the kitchen work surface, a kilner jar is open, and I am counting out wizened red beads for tea. The rosehips (useful for 'all catarrhal, bronchial disorders') have been air-dried until leathery.[1] Against most advice, they haven't been shredded: the seeds and their infinite tiny hairs have not been sifted and separated. Keeping them whole is easier, and, if you're willing to steep them longer, they still release huge quantities of vitamin C. With honey and ginger, they're delicious and comforting.

These rosehips were never supposed to be picked. Three of us went out after dark, no torches, onto the cycle-path behind my friend's house. The lighting there is motion-sensitive, designed to aid cyclists and deter malingerers. In the six o'clock gloom of winter, the tarmac path stretched away in both directions, fading into black. There was a lot of giggling: nervousness and a feeling of transgression as the occasional cyclist zipped past. Picking by touch, we tore our hands up, probably dropped more onto the path than we did into Tupperware, eventually picked the remainder off by the light of a phone. Then we scurried home, drank wine by the fire, and felt brave and united.

Foraging is hardly a secret activity. In Scotland alone, there are a huge number of foraging courses, walks, group workshops. So popular has it become, that Scotland is now promoted as a destination for foraging: Visit Scotland invites the tourist to 'get your hands on these rich pickings of Scottish foraging' in order to participate in the foraging 'renaissance in restaurants and homes'.[2] The Scotsman newspaper published a guide to foraging in Scotland in 2015,

---

1 Law, Donald. *The Concise Herbal Encyclopedia* (New York: St. Martin's, 1976), pp. 81.

2 Clark, Sarah, 'Forage for your supper' Visit Scotland, 4 June 2015. www.visitscotland.com/blog/scotland/foraging/.

complete with recipes.[3] Even Scottish National Heritage encourage foraging as a means of engaging with wild Scotland, writing that 'a growing interest in fresh, seasonal and local food is leading to a revival of wild-harvesting and foraging for ingredients for the table'.[4] This increase in popularity is so great that The Guardian reported it, in 2009, in terms of a gold rush: 'The Forestry Commission estimates that wild harvesting, including harvesting lichens and mosses for natural remedies and horticulture, is worth as much as £21m a year'.[5] This rapid growth comes, of course, with its own difficulties, and has led the Forestry Commission to 'promote wild foods with a code of good practice, to ensure the increasing number of foragers harvest carefully and, where needed, with the landowner's permission'.[6]

So foraging is back. Concerns about ethical food consumption, particularly in terms of global transportation and the working conditions of pickers, have spurred individuals to look locally for their food. This resurgence of interest is also a reaction to urban living, often without adequate green spaces or gardens. Feeling separated from nature, and from the processes of production, has led many people to look once more at what surrounds them. There is also an undeniable cachet to foraging: wild food has become a fashionable commodity. It can be, and indeed is bought, by restaurants at great price, albeit stripped of a certain authenticity. To have been outside, to have got your hands dirty, to own and use something that money can't buy: in a late-capitalist culture, that is prized indeed.

If gathering one's own wild food is not only popular and widespread, but also marketable, then why did we find it so thrilling? What on earth possessed us to do at night what perfectly rational people do on weekends, with rattan baskets and Barbour jackets? It didn't feel like foraging, at least not in the ways that Scottish National Heritage and The Guardian describe, which is not to say that we were doing anything particularly radical, or extraordinary, or that forgetting a torch earns you some sort of brownie points. But, disclaimers aside, what we did that night felt different. Trump was about to be elected. Britain had voted to leave the EU. Scotland was negotiating, once again, to have its voice heard. We were all scared – we are all still scared. We are young women, attempting to

3 Edwards, Ian. 'Wild, Scottish and Free's Guide to Summer Foraging in Scotland', The Scotsman, 10 July 2015. foodanddrink.scotsman.com/food/wild-scottish-and-frees-guide-to-summer-foraging-in-scotland/.

4 'Foraging', Scottish Natural Heritage. www.snh.gov.uk/planning-and-development/economic-value/rural-enterprise/foraging/. Accessed 29 January 2017.

5 Carell, Severin, 'Wild harvest reaps big rewards in foraging rush' The Guardian, 27 April 2009. www.theguardian.com/environment/2009/apr/27/wild-food-foraging-reforesting-scotland.

6 Ibid.

forge careers and lives and to think around big questions whilst the world swings rapidly to the right. Stealing out at night felt like an act of resistance, an act of seizing hold of the world and using it for ourselves. That we could go out, pick rosehips, which we knew the name, shape and qualities of, and then take them home, dry them and use them felt like an incredible gift. Really, it felt quite a lot like magic.

It feels quite a lot like magic that I can write this at all, in fact. Gathering herbs and plants for medicines, sharing them with friends, writing about it, all requires a huge amount of freedom, autonomy and education. After all, for a considerable period in Scotland's history, gathering herbs for medicine or magic, as a woman, could be a serious offence. On the 27th of January, 1591, not far outside Edinburgh, Agnes Sampson was tried as a witch, based on confessions extracted under torture. The list of accusations against her was staggering. Among them, that she 'healed by witchcraft Johnne Thomsoune in Dirletoun, though he remained a cripple' and that she 'cured Johnne Peiny in Preston by prayer and incantation'.[7] Most probably, she used herbs and plants gathered from the surrounding countryside.

Agnes Sampson was a midwife and local 'wise woman'. She offered counsel and natural medicine to those in her community who could not afford extortionate doctors fees. Such women (and indeed, men), whose presence had been part of village life for centuries, came under attack during the professionalisation of medicine in the sixteenth century. 'Wise women and their medicines', historian Andrew Wear writes, 'were often scoffed at by professionally trained doctors, nearly always male, who were anxious to protect their professional status'.[8] The skills of wise women and other local healers were minimised and dismissed, but their trade did not diminish. Many of their practices have since been debunked by contemporary medicine, such as widespread adherence to the 'doctrine of signatures', the belief that 'natural objects that looked like a part of the body could cure diseases that would arise there'. However, many of their cures were effective, as Wear notes, they included 'many naturally occurring ingredients that are medically useful'.[9] So, when dismissal of wise women failed to work, it was easier to vilify them.

It is not much of a step, after all, to suggest that healing skill is not healing at all, but witchcraft. Agnes Sampson would have foraged, gathering what she needed from hedgerows to heal those who came to her. For this, she was forced

7 '27 January 1591 Trial of Agnes Sampson', Ryerson University. www.ryerson.ca/~meinhard/sampson. html. Accessed 29 January 2017.

8 Wear, A., Knowledge and Practice in English Medicine, 1500 – 1800 (Cambridge: Cambridge University Press, 2000)

9 Ibid.

to wear the Witch's Bridle, an iron headdress with four metal spikes that were inserted into her mouth so that speaking pierced her tongue and cheeks. She had all of her body hair shaved off by male interrogators in an attempt to find her 'witches' mark', and after several days of torture, confessed to being in league with the devil, and gave the names of others who were as well. She was, of course, only one of a huge number of women who were put to death during the witch trials of Scotland.[10]

The resurgence of foraging glosses over these historical connotations with witchcraft, precisely because foraging is now primarily associated with food. Access to free, reliable medicine has overturned the need for home remedies, and even these can be bought in 'alternative therapy' shops, dispensed by experts. Foraging, at least as portrayed in the mainstream media, is a middle-class leisure pursuit, rather than a matter of survival. And whilst it is fun to make wild garlic pesto, or to stew windfall apples, or to make elderflower cordial, it is impossible to pretend that these activities do not have historically gender and class-based implications.

There are, however, projects and individuals who are broadening perspectives on foraging, and respecting its nature as a historical practice. The Rhynie Woman collective, Debbi Beeson and Daisy Williamson, based in the North East of Scotland, and are engaged with promoting awareness of regional heritage through foraging practices. A recent project for Deveron Arts, 'Cooking the Landscape', saw them 'utilising foraging, honouring local food, traditional recipes and celebrations—to create a platform which promoted dialogue, skill sharing, and the exchange of ideas'.[11] Rhynie Woman collective do not just forage: they engage with historic, local practices around gathering and preparation. By acknowledging the traditions that surround them, they are better able to understand foraging as a situated practice, and one that can enrich knowledge of local heritage. For the 'Cooking the Landscape' project, they took as a guiding quotation Michael Pollan's statement that 'the shared meal elevates eating from a mechanical process of fuelling the body to a ritual of family and community, from the mere animal biology to an act of culture'.[12] By re-introducing the idea of gathering, preparing and eating food as ritual practice, Rhynie Woman are able to explore and honour foraging traditions.

There is something mystical, magical about their foraging and cooking. They pose questions about wild foods and hospitality: 'What does it say of the host when served stinging nettles for tea; hidden inside a cream cake, their threat

10 'The Survey of Scottish Witchcraft', The University of Edinburgh School of History, Classics and Archeology. www.shca.ed.ac.uk/Research/witches/introduction.html. Accessed 29 January 2017.

11 Deveron-Projects, www.deveron-projects.com/rhynie-woman/. Accessed 29 January 2017.

12 Ibid.

to sting ones tongue still present, lurking'.[13] Stinging nettles here are not being recognised for their culinary, or medicinal use, but rather for their symbolic potency. To eat a stinging nettle is to suffer pain, to be scolded for speaking out of turn, perhaps. It has the feeling of a punishment, or a curse – or even an echo of the Witch's Bridle. Of course, the true benignity of nettles – excellent for cleansing the blood – is here less important than their folkloric, symbolic impact. There is also the ripple of distrust that still spreads, even hundreds of years after Agnes Sampson's trial. 'What does it say of the host?' they ask: can we trust women who pick wild nettles not to hurt us, not to harbour and harness strange, wild power?

This strange, wild power might be frightening to those who eat the nettles, but it is important for those who gather them. I am aware, as I sort herbs or learn about mushrooms, or read a friend's tarot, that perhaps what I am primarily interested in is power. Power against the constant, disempowering experience of being a woman. Power against catcallers, rapists, Presidents who believe that sexual assault is acceptable. Power to see the future, or help a cold, or ease the winter blues, precisely because I have so little power in other areas. My tinctures will not break glass ceilings; my spells will not help women get the abortions they need, or equal pay, or anything else. But foraging in hedgerows and doing small magic with friends who I love feels empowering. It is like holding a secret in the warmth of your ribcage, and letting it glow right through you. And I am braver, I think, because of it. Because I am part of a community of strong women, finding ways to make ourselves powerful. I am braver in interviews, in meetings, in pitching for articles and negotiating boundaries. It is not in the least surprising that as the world seems to swing to the right, as the days seem to grow darker, that women are turning back to hedgerow magic, to attempting forms of community and ritual as part of working out how to fight back, how to remain empowered.

There are some places in Britain where hedge-magic and foraging for healing has never really gone away. In Cornwall, a strong tradition of Paganism and wise women persists. Cassandra Latham-Jones, for example, is the village wise woman of the Cornish village of St Buryan.[14] She offers a range of services, from creating charms with natural ingredients to counselling individuals who need help. Latham-Jones is a celebrant, tarot reader, and witch. In a filmed interview for the Open University's 'Religion Today' course, the camera follows Latham-Jones as she walks through the Cornish countryside, identifying plants to create a protection spell. Down-to-earth and entirely practical about her

13 Ibid.

14 Latham-Jones, Cassandra, Grumpy Old Witchcraft, www.grumpyoldwitchcraft.com/. Accessed 29 January 2017.

magic, Latham-Jones refers to herself as a 'village witch', because it is the 'most relatable term', and says that she is asked about similar things that witches were asked about centuries ago: health, careers, romance.[15] Latham-Jones is dressed in black, and wears a black hat. She lives in a stone cottage, is married to a woman, and openly practices magic. In many ways, she is the epitome of Otherness, and yet she exists amid a community, serving their needs. Whether or not this community have an uneasy relationship with Latham-Jones is not discussed: the documentary and her website focus on the positive aspects of her practice. Latham-Jones does not conform to heteronormative ideals of femininity: she wears no makeup, wears masculine clothing and her magic does not relate to the domestic. She lives outside societal expectations, and is frank about the difficulty of making a living with her work.

Whilst she may not, therefore, be a traditional role model, she is nevertheless a very appealing figure. She is clearly passionate about her work, and feels empowered to live a life in accordance with her own desires and virtues, rather than those of society. Latham-Jones is an important figure in terms of the re-association of foraging with magic, and in terms of situating it historically. She is testament to the fact that foraging has been a traditionally female practice, associated with ritual and magic, not simple a leisure pursuit or interesting hobby.

By deliberately revitalising understanding of foraging as a radical, historically dangerous act, associated with arcane female knowledge and power, we can understand its potential as a feminist practice. Information about the landscape has, since the professionalisation of botany during the Victorian period, been primarily written and distributed by men. Male writers such as Tim Dee and Robert MacFarlane have spearheaded the current resurgence in nature writing over the past decade. Their approach to the natural world is that of the scientist or explorer: travelling through and documenting what is seen. Whilst bodily engagement with the landscape in these books is inevitable, there is no sense of engaging with the land in terms of what it produces. Picking berries, learning about the properties of different plants is secondary to the more scholarly concerns of the area's history and geography. Narrative immersion in landscape is engaging, and necessary in order to draw attention to our current environmental crisis, but the new nature writing can often be self-centred. A journey across mountains is, more often than not, related as a journey of self-discovery. This self-discovery is interesting and informative, but it obscures landscape as a site of plenty and bounty. Instead, it turns the focus back onto the male author and his adventuring.

---

15 Woodland Wanderer, 'Open University Religion Today Cassandra Latham Village Witch', YouTube, 21 April 2011. www.youtube.com/watch?v=h77DjKOZ3Z4

Although she does not discuss foraging, Scottish nature writer Nan Shepherd, whose face was recently put onto the Scottish five pound note, radically refigures traditional nature writing tropes in her book The Living Mountain. Rather than walking through hills as an observer, Shepherd 'a localist of the best kind', seeks to communicate her 'acute perception' of the Cairngorm range.[16] Rather than walking 'up' the mountains, she walks instead 'into' them. Dissolving the ego, Shepherd seeks to be absorbed into the landscape, to understand it not through the accretion of knowledge but through direct haptic experience. She wishes to see, and become the mountain at the same time. Described by Macfarlane as a 'part-time mystic', interested in esoteric religions and Zen Buddhism, Shepherd has a quality of 'Otherness'. Not logical but emotional, not academic but perceptive, she is described in similar terms to wise women such as Latham-Jones. Rejecting an objective approach to her surroundings, she instead favoured immersion, intuitive understanding and repeated visits. The mountains, for Shepherd, were animate, and rather than learning about them, they taught her. This interest in walking, her enjoyment of isolation, the fact that she did not marry, all indicate an Otherness that seems to be held in common with other 'mystic' women. Any choice that removes them from the dominant cultural narratives and expectations placed upon them imbues these women with a sense that they are dangerous, somehow. They are the hostesses who might, perhaps, serve nettles.

So I stand in the shadow of all of these women. I do not face persecution like Agnes Martin; I do not have as much knowledge as Cassandra Latham-Jones. But I feel that any woman who decides to step outside what is demanded of her owes a debt to witches, to wise women, to women who walk alone in the hills. I am learning, from encylopedias, from Tumblr, from friends and family. It does not matter if what I am doing is mostly nonsense, entirely nonsense, or not nonsense at all. What matters is that foraging connects me to the land and to friends, takes me outside, makes me look. Learning about the plants that grow around me, and how they might be used, lets me walk through my city with my eyes open. Preparing teas and drying herbs and burning red candles gives me a sense of power. Perhaps it is an illusion, or perhaps it is busy-work, or perhaps I really am doing magic.

The three of us felt so alive picking rosehips. Alive is how I want to feel, how rootling around in bushes or setting my intentions makes me feel. Feeling connected to the seasons, to the natural world, to the rhythms of growth and decay is helpful, grounding, reminds us that we are not alone on earth. There is beauty and bounty around us, if we look for it, and perhaps that is all the

16 Macfarlane, Robert, 'Introduction', The Living Mountain, Nan Shepherd, (Edinburgh: Cannongate, 2011)

magic we need. Or perhaps, what we need is real magic, whether that comes in the form of resistance and community or the form of blackthorn charms and skullcap tinctures, and howling up at the moon.

———————————————————————

That was an essay from 404 Ink's debut book Nasty Women, *a collection of essays and accounts on what it is to be a woman in the 21st century, published on International Women's Day, March 8th 2017.*

BIOGRAPHIES

CONTRIBUTOR BIOGRAPHIES

Chris Beausang was born in Dublin. He is currently investigating the resurgence of literary modernism the work of Anne Enright, Eimear McBride and Will Self as part of his doctoral research. He has been published in *Gorse*, *The Bohemyth* and *The Galway Review*. He is working on his first novel.

Chris Boyland is forty-four years old and lives and works in central Scotland. He is a published poet – most recently, in the anthology *Aiblins: New Scottish Political Poetry*, available from Luath Press and regularly appears at poetry and spoken word nights around Glasgow.

Paul Bristow writes children's fiction, folktales and comics, sometimes all at once. His debut children's book *The Superpower Project* was shortlisted for the Kelpies prize and published in 2016. Paul also runs literacy social enterprise, Magic Torch Comics, which encourages the use of comics and graphic novels in schools.

Rex Bromfield was a feature film writer/director for many years with his first film *Love At First Sight*, invited to Filmex by The American Film Institute. He ran an educational software company winning the Newmedia Invision Award, Newsweek's Editor's Choice Award and Parenting Magazine's Magic Software Award for preschool app Paint 'N' Play.

Ricky Monahan Brown's fiction has been published in many magazines and journals, and Freight Books' *Umbrellas of Edinburgh*. Ricky has performed with his band Nerd Bait at the Edinburgh International Book Festival and the Edinburgh International Science Festival. He is the co-producer of the spoken word and music night Interrobang?!
@ricky_ballboy / apoplectic.me (Personal work)
@InterrobangEdin / interrobang.scot (Interrobang)
@NerdBaitBand / nerdbaitband.com (Band)

Jen Burrows works in TV drama, writing poetry behind the scenes. She's also a music blogger, bookworm and feminist fuelled by green tea.
Twitter: @girlglitch

Ria Cagampang is an Oxford based writer who has also been blogging, in various forms, for the past six years. When not fighting the patriarchy online, offline, she works in Digital Marketing within educational publishing.
Twitter: @RCagz
ThoroughlyModernMillennial.com

Eva Carson was born in Glasgow in 1984. Her work is particularly influenced by horror, science fiction, and the voices and landscapes of Scotland. She is working on her first novel. She also sends a monthly newsletter about fiction and other strange things. You can subscribe to it here: tinyletter.com/evacarson.
Twitter: @eva_carson1

Celeste W. Clark is a born & raised Edinburger and recently graduated illustrator who studied at Leith School of Art and Edinburgh College of art. She is interested in comics (why do they always end up being about hair and water?), religious iconography and cute animals.
Instagram: @cwc_illustration
cwc.illustration.com

Siobhan Dunlop is a writer, book blogger, and recent Masters graduate, with a liking for bad rhymes and unnecessary literary references. She writes prose and poetry, talks about books and reviews upcoming publications on her blog, and volunteers for Oxfam and at her local library.
Twitter: @fiendfull
fiendfullyreading.tumblr.com

Alan Fielden is an Anglo-Korean writer and theatre maker. His plays have been described as "Ingenious" (The Independent), and "[possessing] a richness of thought" (Exeunt). His fiction and poetry have appeared in *Minor Literatures*, *The Literateur*, *Der Grief*, and *Allotrope Press*. In 2014 he wrote 99 plays in as many days [99plays.tumblr.com].
Twitter: @afielden
alanfielden.co.uk

C[F]ameron Foster is a cultural dogsbody based in Leith. He is co-host of the Flint & Pitch Revue with Jenny Lindsay and part of Morven Cunningham's

LeithLate team. He is also a freelance graphic designer and now, apparently, fancies himself as some kind of poet.

Lucy Holden is a young writer from Chicago. Currently her life's mission is to explore every inch of the world around her so that she can better understand people and their cultures. That is why she is now making her way teaching English from the small Silesian city of Gliwice, Poland. When she's not off having adventures, she spends her time jamming with friends, writing, baking bread, and reading Tolstoy.

Suzey Ingold is a writer, linguist and coffee addict, currently based in Edinburgh, Scotland. Brought up in a household where children's books are quoted over the dinner table, literature has always had a strong influence on her life. She enjoys travelling, scented candles and brunch.
Twitter: @suzeysays
suzeysays.com

Nadine Aisha Jassat is the author of *Still*, a feminist poetry pamphlet. She has performed solo shows at the Edinburgh Fringe Festival, Just festival, and Audacious Women's Festival, and is Writer in Residence for The Young Women's Movement. Her essay 'On Naming' is included in 404 Ink's *Nasty Women*.
Twitter: @nadineaishaj
nadineaisha.wixsite.com/nadineaisha

Veronique Kootstra is originally from the Netherlands but writes and dreams in English. She loves the challenge of flash fiction but has recently started exploring longer forms and is working on her first novel. She is part of the Write Like a Grrrl community.
Twitter: @vkootstra

Hannah Lavery is a writer and performer from Edinburgh, who has made her home in Dunbar. Hannah runs CoastWord Festival in Dunbar and was Scottish Book Trust Reader In Residence for East Lothian in 2015. She is also the founding member of the writing collective, The Writing Mums.

Katy Lennon is a sci-fi and horror writer living in Edinburgh. She writes about the future, posthumanism, AI and social media, birthed from an obsession with internet culture. Sex and technology are recurring themes, and her fascination with the two frequently combine. Previous work can be found in Shoreline of Infinity. Twitter: @blooood_bath

Jenny Lindsay is a spoken word poet, writer and performer based in Edinburgh and is also the director of Flint & Pitch Productions. 'THIS SCRIPT' was commissioned for the Return Flight MEL > EDI project, in partnership with Going Down Swinging.

Kirsty Logan is a professional daydreamer. She is the author of two story collections, *A Portable Shelter* and *The Rental Heart & Other Fairytales*, and a novel, *The Gracekeepers*. She lives in Glasgow with her wife and their rescue dog. She has tattooed toes.

Rugadh **Calum L MacLeòid** ann an Inbhir Nis agus tha e a' fuireach ann am Montréal. Ann an 2014 choisinn e Duais nan Sgrìobhadairean ùra aig Comhairle nan Leabhraichean agus Urras Leabhraichean na h-Alba. Bidh e cuideachd a' sgrìobhadh colbh Gàidhlig anns a' phàipear naidheachd The National.

Calum L MacLeod was born in Inverness and now lives in Montréal. In 2014 he won a New Writers Award from the Scottish Book Trust and the Gaelic Books Council. He also writes the Gaelic column for The National.

Colm Macqueen is a freelance translator and writer from the seaside village of Fairlie in North Ayrshire. When not deciphering German medical reports, Spanish film synopses, Dutch birth certificates or French biographies, he enjoys creative writing in English and Gaelic, ice hockey, organic gardening and jogging with his dog Oscar.
Twitter: @cmacq1
colmmacqueen.wordpress.com

Stevie McEwan is Scottish but since he can't stand racists or Tories, for now he lives in Oman with his family. In his free time he sits in the desert and contemplates square slice and pineapple cakes.

Chris McQueer is a 20-something year old writer and sales assistant from Glasgow. Chris kept his writing a secret from his friends and family for several months before his girlfriend, Vanessa, encouraged him to share his work through Twitter (@ChrisMcQueer). His debut short story collection *Hings* will be published by 404 Ink in July 2017.

Helen Victoria Murray is a writer, poet and literary critic, concerned with subjective experience; fleshly and ephemeral things. She is a current MRes candidate at the University of Glasgow, specialising in Neo-Victorian literature

and culture. She has been published in several journals, including *The Bohemyth* and *The Rising Phoenix Review*.
Twitter: @HelenVMurray
helenvictoriamurray.wordpress.com

Heather Parry is a writer and editor who lives in Edinburgh. She writes dark, surrealist short fiction and is currently working on her first novel.
Twitter: @heatherparryuk
heatherparry.com

Errol Rivera is an Edinburgh-based American genre writer and freelance academic. Scotland's givin'm a lot – he's intent on returning the favour. He's into co-writing novels and has a couple coming out soon. His writing, teaching, and research are about young people, empathy, and inventing things.
Twitter: @escottrivera

Jeffrey G. Roberts is a graduate of Northern Arizona University, and has been published in various genres. He has two novels on Amazon: *The Healer* and *Cherries in Winter*. He lives in Tucson, Arizona, USA.
Twitter: @talejotter
Atalespinner.weebly.com.

Mhairi M. Robertson illustrates books for children and is the accidental creator of #MhairiComics on Instagram, drawn for her own amusement on her daily commute to and from work. The comics chronicle the everyday events of her life at home and work and, occasionally, as her comical alter ego, Art Ninja.

Tom Paul Smith is from England and works as a TV sports producer. He has a degree in Film Production from Southampton University and Cinematography from Victoria Motion Picture School in Canada. He now lives in Abu Dhabi – as he works better on sand.

Claire Squires is Professor of Publishing Studies at the University of Stirling, and a Scottish Book Trust New Writer 2015 Awardee. She's currently writing a YA novel, *Fire Fall*.
Twitter: @clairesquires
clairesquires.com

Michael Stephenson lives in Bathgate. His poems have previously appeared in a number of publications including *New Writing Scotland*, *Gutter* and *Poetry Scotland*.

Alice Tarbuck is a writer and researcher based in Edinburgh. She is completing a PhD on poet and visual artist Thomas A. Clark. Recent publications appear in *Dangerous Women*, *Antiphon*, *Zarf* and *Three Drops from the Cauldron*. She is part of Edinburgh writers collective content work produce form.
Twitter: @atarbuck

Rhiannon Tate is a graphic designer and illustrator who started out making award winning feature length animations and documentaries. Tea fiend and Japanophile, she loves travelling, stormy weather and the sea. She now lives in Edinburgh marketing her partner's business, writing stories and drawing comics when no-one is looking.
Twitter: @sephryngrey
teawolf.co.uk

L. A. Traynor is the author of *Anomalies and Revelations*. Her poetry has been published in several national anthologies, websites and magazines. She is on the committee of Federation of Writers (Scotland) and member of Scottish Writers' Centre. She supports the development of Poetry Films under Fierce Poetry in Motion.
Facebook: L A Traynor/Lesley Traynor
Twitter: @latraynor & @motionpoets

Simon Ward is a Liverpool-based writer of contemporary fairy tales. His stories have been published in *Offline Samizdat*, *SAND*, *HARK* and *Streets of Berlin: An Anthology*. In addition to fiction, he writes reviews of events for *Corridor8*. He also facilitates workshops for local charities, such as Writing on the Wall.

Thomas Welsh is a 36 year old Glasgow based writer. He was the winner of the Elbow Room short story competition in early 2017 and was shortlisted for the Glimmer Train prize. His first novel *Anna Undreaming* will be published by Owl Hollow in January 2018.
Twitter: @calmdowntom
www.calmdowntom.com

THANK YOU

THANK YOU TO OUR PATRONS

Some of these fine folk supported 404 Ink before there was even a mention of a magazine and some of them more recently jumped on board after reading and (we hope) loving the first issue. By pledging an amount of money per issue, they are helping us get the 404 ship sailing so we can get a lot of lovely artists and writers into print and pay them all for their hard work. For that we are eternally grateful. Give a big round of applause to:

Sophia Althammer
Nicola Balkind
Russell Barker
Chris Boyland
Alistair Braidwood
Nicole Brandon
Rachel Branson
Charlene Busalli
Caroline Clarke
Sean Cleaver
Robert Clyde
Suzanne Connor
Catriona Cox
Muireann Crowley
P. C. Dettmann
Gwendlyn Drayton
Finbarr Farragher
Madeleine Fenner
Liz Fox
Claire Genevieve
Morven Gow
Lor Graham
Sinéad Grainger
Robbie Guillory
Kris Haddow
Rosie Howie
Michaela Hunter

Inside The Bell Jar
Sarah-Louise Kelly
Peter Kerr
Rebecca Kleanthous
Kirstin Lamb
Jennie May
Susan McIvor
Mairi McKay
Kerry McShane
Jamie Norman
Daiden O'Regan
Almond Press
Samantha Quy
Shell
EK Reeder
Simon Rowberry
Victoria Sinden
Kirstyn Smith
Claire Squires
Elizabeth Stanley
Kirsty Stanley
Emma Swann
Nicole Sweeney
Kristin Walter
Aran Ward Sell
Stevie Williams
Mark Wrightman
Ashley Wyse
Emma Zetterström

And a number of patrons who choose to remain anonymous.

We love you guys.

Seriously.

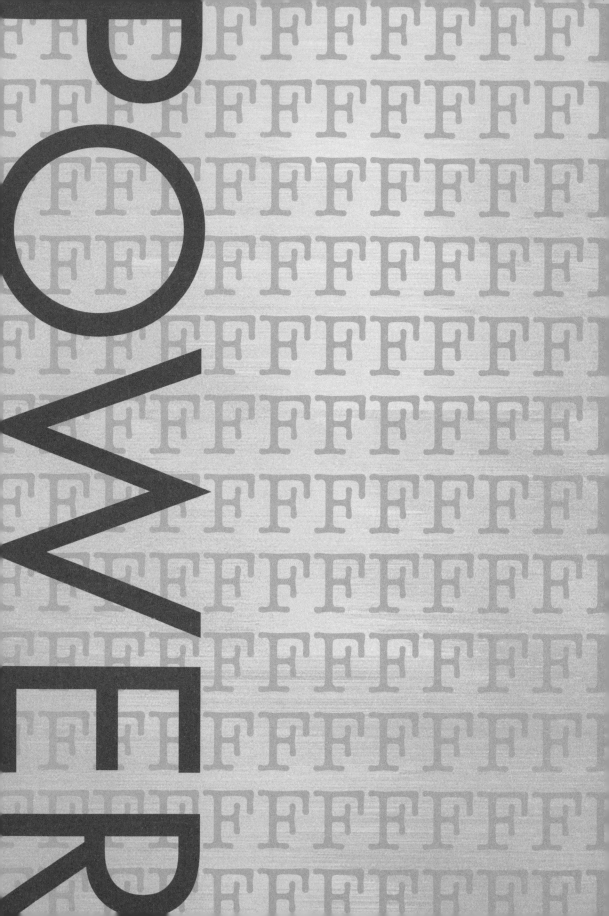

ISSUE 3: POWER

We would say third time lucky, but that would imply that the first two issues of 404 were unlucky, and well – that's simply not true. Following on from Error and the F-Word, we'll be ending this particular trilogy by exploring Power.

Power struggles?
Power plays?
Super powers?
Powers of the electrical variety?
The political variety?
Maybe even the magical variety?

Okay, okay. You get the idea.

So, if you're a fiction writer or poet in English, Scots or Scottish Gaelic, a comic artist, or have a non-fiction piece you think should be shared in relation to these particularly powerful themes, we want to hear from you.

Our submission guidelines and dates can be found at 404ink.com/submissions. You could be in our next issue. Great, huh?

SUBSCRIBE TO 404 INK

We really love crowdfunding and are currently using the crowdfunding platform Patreon as a means of offering a subscription service to this twice-yearly magazine.

If you enjoyed the first two issues of 404 Ink, would like to be signed up for the third, and receive all the gossip and info about upcoming publications first, then Patreon is the place to be!

How does Patreon work?

So glad you asked. On Patreon you pledge to give a creator a chosen amount of money either per month or per creation. We currently have our Patreon set up so we receive all pledges when the magazine issue is complete and ready to be sent out to readers. This is twice a year, in summer and winter.

You can pledge $1 to receive all the behind-the-scenes updates before anyone else, $5 for the ebook, $10 for the printed magazine (UK only) or $20 for the printed magazine if you're outside of the UK. (Patreon is a US company so pledges are in dollars, but they convert the currency, and it works wherever you are in the world!). All patrons are the first to hear about any news or reveals we may have.

When we're ready to send the magazine to subscribers we press the big red button which will send all pledged money to us – unlike normal subscriptions, we don't see any money until the magazine's ready, so you're not paying for anything until we have it ready for you in all its glory.

So why Patreon?

We're using Patreon because it's a public platform that brings transparency and accountability to the creative process. It means we have a direct relationship with our readers, we know that there's money coming in to help us pay our authors and it spreads the word about all those talented folks. We hope you'll hop on board.

WWW.PATREON.COM/404INK

ABOUT 404 INK

ABOUT 404 INK

404 Ink is an alternative and independent book and literary magazine publisher based in the UK. We look to publish the weirder and wilder fiction, non-fiction, poetry and comics out there in our magazine, in English, Scots and Scottish Gaelic. New issues are released in summer and winter every year. You can subscribe to the magazine through Patreon (flick back a page for more info on that) or buy single issues from our website (below).

We're always on the lookout for novels, short story collections, narrative nonfiction, and graphic novels and we accept unsolicited submissions. Drop by our website for full information on submissions and more: www.404ink.com

Find/follow/like us at all the usual places:

Facebook: /404ink
Twitter: @404ink
Instagram: 404ink

GOODBYE